GATE TO THE HEART

GATE TO THE HEART

A Manual of Contemplative Jewish Practice

RABBI ZALMAN M. SCHACHTER-SHALOMI

Edited by
NETANEL MILES-YÉPEZ
ROBERT MICHA'EL ESFORMES

Albion
Andalus
Boulder, Colorado
2013

*"The old shall be renewed,
and the new shall be made holy."*

— Rabbi Avraham Yitzhak Kook

Albion-Andalus, Inc.
P. O. Box 19852
Boulder, CO 80308
www.albionandalus.com

Design and layout by Albion-Andalus Books

Cover design by Sari Wisenthal-Shore

Cover art "Shiviti of Moshe Galanti" by Netanel Miles-Yépez

Charcoal drawing, "Rabbi Zalman Schachter-Shalomi," page xii, by Netanel Miles-Yépez

Illustration, "Shiviti," page 37, designed by Zalman M. Schachter-Shalomi and executed by Henri Mugier

Other illustrations by Netanel Miles-Yépez

ISBN-13: 978-0615944562 (Albion-Andalus Books)

ISBN-10: 0615944566

In Memoriam

These people are fondly
And reverently remembered.
May they intercede on our behalf,
And may their souls be bound up
In the vortex of life:

My *rebbe,*
Rabbi Yosef Yitzhak Schneersohn,
Dr. Sheila Cantor, Rev. John Dixon Copp,
Gerald Heard, David Jackson, Rabbi Gedaliah Kenig,
Rivka Bat Sarah v'Selim Menaged, Michael Ross,
Rabbi Moshe Tchekhoval, and Rev. Howard Thurman.

Contents

Gate to the Heart

Introduction to the Ladder of Traditional Prayer

Ritual Objects in Judaism

The Bedtime Sh'ma'

Acknowledgments

THIS BOOK WOULD NOT have come to light without the help of Aaron Claman, Father Dave Denny, Esther Ekus, Harvey Ekus, Robert Micha'el Esformes, Melvin Fenson, Tirzah Firestone, David Friedman, Thomas Hast, Ruth Hirsch, Eve Ilsen, Lynne Iser, David Jackson, Ruth Gan Kagan, Phil Labowitz, Shoni Labowitz, Netanel Miles-Yépez, Florence Ross, Deane Shapiro, Diane Sharon, Richard Siegel, Mickey Singer, Michael Strassfeld, Sharon Strassfeld, Bobbie Zelkind, and the folks at Lama Foundation. May they be blessed in all things.

— Z.M.S-S.

Retrospect

IN THE LATE 1950's, while still a Hillel director at the University of Manitoba, I became heavily involved in showing young people how to *davven;* that is to say, how to pray contemplatively with intention and insight. Their interest was such that I began to introduce them to Hasidic contemplative practices for redeeming prayer and worship from mere recitation, techniques that I had first learned as a Habad-Lubavitcher Hasid. Thus I began to think that it might be nice to have a little meditation manual in English that described these practices.

I began to pray and meditate on this, until finally, in 1958, I wrote a small booklet called *The First Step: A Primer of a Jew's Spiritual Life* (not to be confused with my later book, *First Steps to a New Jewish Spirit*). It simply poured through me, almost as if it were being dictated, and I quickly sent off a draft to the Lubavitcher Rebbe, Rabbi Menachem Mendel Schneerson, *z'l,* for his approval. He responded positively (with some suggestions for an appended bibliography) and soon after, I printed a small pocket edition with the help of the late David Jackson of Chicago and Melvin Fenson.

In those years, I used to furnish the people who wrote to me for guidance on how to deepen their interest in Jewish spirituality with a 'kit' containing *The First Step*, to help with the 'how,' and my translation of Rebbe Nahman of Bratzlav's *Meshivat Nefesh,* to help with the 'why,' and to offer them some encouragement.

That first pocket edition went through several printings and changes, until finally, in 1965, it became a section in *The First Jewish Catalog,* created by some of my students. Over the years, I too went through several editions and changes, and after much God-wrestling, both inside and outside of Judaism, I decided in the early 1990s to update the book to make it more consistent with my current outlook.

In doing this, I received generous help in time and energy from Dr. Diane Sharon, who interviewed me, transcribed our talks, and edited them into a more colloquial version called, *Sha'ar El HaLev: A Gate to the Heart* (1991), which was printed for use in the Wisdom School I ran with my wife, Eve Ilsen. Later, Robert Micha'el Esformes—a gifted *hazzan* and *ba'al te'fillah*—labored on this manuscript, editing and formatting into an elegant new edition called, *Gate to the Heart: An Evolving Process* (1993), which we made available on a limited basis to people involved with Jewish renewal. Now, my student, Netanel Miles-Yépez has taken it upon himself to edit and publish a new edition of the book, correcting errors and incorporating suggestions from Ruth Gan Kagan and Robert Micha'el Esformes.

This small manual is to help you connect with your own heart, the Heart of the World, and the Heart of God. Treat its method as a stimulating helper, not as a set of rails on which you *must* travel. Your own aroused heart and awakened consciousness, responding to the promptings of your own soul and a loving Providence, will tell you when to ignore the text and surrender to the grace which, in working with the book, you have been prepared to receive and cherish.

With thanksgiving to God, I offer this manual as a guide and as a reminder to enliven your prayer-life.

— Zalman Schachter-Shalomi, Boulder, Colorado,
24 Tevet, the *yahrzeit* of R' Shneur Zalman of Liadi

A NOTE ON LANGUAGE

LANGUAGE IS OFTEN an impediment in spiritual work. We need a new kind of language, one that has inter-active tenses. Rather than, 'I'm sitting on a chair, and the chair is being sat upon,' we might say that we are 'inter-sitting'! This is a far more accurate way of looking at a situation, and can actually help us re-frame many of the limited notions that keep us stuck with regard to religion.

Likewise, we have 'he,' 'she,' and 'it.' How do we move beyond specific gender? How do we talk about God? There are no words yet. Languages are very reluctant to change and don't yield easily to neologisms. Language has not even caught-up with some of our most basic realizations of the past. For example, to say 'sunrise' and 'sunset,' as we know, is a mistake. If we were to say, 'earth turning to receive its daily portion of sunshine,' that would be more correct. Just speaking about it in this way would create different possibilities. We would be reminded that when it is dark, the sun is shining on the other side of the globe.

— Z.M.S-S.

Introduction to
Aspects of the Spiritual Path
& Jewish Mysticism

To Whom This Might Concern

I WANT TO BEGIN by saying that this endeavor is one of mutuality. For even now we are sharing an experience of reading and being read; the thoughts that move me to write this at this moment are also moving you as you read. In this way, this manual has both its origin and fulfillment in *our* present, in the 'now' shared by both of us. It is in the nature of this manual's beginning that our partnership will become clear by its end.

This is a manual written to give you practical information on entering an intentional Jewish spiritual discipline. If you have taken up this text, I can assume you are attempting to re-engage or respond to and express nascent spiritual stirrings in yourself, hoping to develop the holy source within you. Whether you are new to this quest or not does not matter; we are all beginners in every moment of the spiritual journey. You may have read various books on spiritual matters previously, both Jewish and non-Jewish, and perhaps have even entered into practices to realize in spirit what has been suggested in print. It is likely that you already trust in the existence of the *Greater Reality*, though your efforts to enter into communion with It may have been only partially successful.

If you are looking to continue this pursuit in the context of a Jewish meditative discipline that is both ancient and modern, and are concerned enough to invest time and effort in working on yourself, it is for you that I have written this small introduction to Jewish meditation and contemplation.

This work is *spiritual* not *mental*, and therefore, you need not bring to it a clearly crystallized philosophy. All you need is a focused willingness to test some of the beliefs you already hold, and some you wish to hold, in the laboratory of your experience. (If you find yourself struggling with the questions of philosophy and theology, read the reflection on these in the Appendices.)

Allocate for yourself a time-budget of at least a half-hour each day, and an additional two hours each week for this work. It should be done with regularity, and preferably, at a fixed time (or fixed times) of the day. A trusted friend with whom you can practice and discuss this work is also valuable, for spiritual work done in loneliness, without interpersonal reality checks, will often breed unhelpful fantasies and lead to ego-inflation. A more experienced practitioner is a very helpful ally on the path.

Enter this gate prepared to experience profound changes; but recognize that in order to make progress in this work, a certain level-headed sobriety is also necessary. Patterns of long standing will exert their inertia, impeding your effort. Unusual stirrings and occurrences may threaten your equilibrium. Rapture is not the only experience to anticipate, nor is easy progress certain; but be assured that real effort will be rewarded.

Just as plants are heliotropic beings, growing toward the Sun, so we humans (and all of creation) are Theotropic beings, growing toward God. Thus, there are basic similarities in all methods of spiritual direction. The approach used here, however, is that of classical Jewish mysticism, as refined by Hasidism, and particularly by the Habad school. For this reason, we will use a fair amount of Hebrew terminology in transliteration.

When you have gained proficiency in the exercises outlined here, you will need a teacher or guide to prescribe the next steps for you. There are teachers who can take you further; but further steps cannot be given in a manual, since it cannot speak to your specific needs. Here, it is enough to introduce to you some elementary techniques from the spiritual 'laboratory' of Judaism.

In order to minimize confusion, it is suggested that, for the time being, you discontinue the reading of other manuals of practice. Later, with the experience of the fruits of practice, reading other texts will be useful. The various states described will then, perhaps, be more familiar to you, and will serve as validation for your own experience. But, until you gain that additional experience, focus on this method exclusively.

During this time, inspirational reading (rather than theoretical material) will be of great importance. To keep the soul moist and the ego in a humble state, stories of those who have loved God are very useful. Choose such stories and read them slowly and regularly over many days, prefacing your practice with these readings. Ask God that your reading inspire your continued effort. Before you put the book away, think back and fasten what you have read in your memory. Savor a phrase and repeat it a few times with each breath. Ask your body to move to it, and then conclude the session, anchoring the inspiration in your bones and blood.

In your choice of material, books describing the thoughts and lives of the *tzaddikim*, the 'righteous ones,' can help to keep your motivation strong and focused. Poetry that speaks of the love of God is also very useful. However, do not at this point consider the functional aspects of the literature, only its inspirational effect. Also, note in your choice of texts that the saints of the past sometimes achieved their legendary stature at the expense of a wider human integration. Today, we are aiming less at heroic feats of asceticism and more at the balanced growth of the whole person.

I offer prayers for your success. *Amen.*

STAGES OF THE PATH

Spiritual progress is often charted in linear stages, though the actual experience of these is usually more dynamic and organically unique to the individual seeker. However, a linear progression is useful for teaching, so I like to speak of five such stages.[*]

The first is the Rung of Love, fueled by the neophyte's enthusiasm. Optimistic, grateful for new light and growing joy, it overlooks the difficulties ahead. But many are caught in a loop here, moving from one path to another on the same level, all in order to continue enjoying the thrill of newness and the sweet emotion of discovery. Fortunately, the newness wears off and the thrill eventually evaporates. It necessarily ends in order to propel movement to the next stage.

The Rung of Power is the level of mastery of the medium, the technique. At this stage of rigorous discipline, one develops a new center of gravity, a place of personal power, inspired by an initial understanding of the inner-light through focused mastery of the medium. Such is the power of this rung. At this stage, one has to be careful not to get caught-up

---

[*] Based on Dr. Karl Stern's adaptation of Freud's five stages of pyscho-sexual development to religious practice.

in a practice of ascetic-athletics and over-strictness, which is often accompanied by intolerance of 'weaker' others.

Having found the limitations of the Rung of Power, we ascend to the Rung of Beauty, a level in which symbols are highly charged and new depths of meaning suggest themselves in emotional creativity. Here, at the gate of Beauty, the various dramas between the soul and her Source are revealed. Here, God is the Parent, the Friend, or the Beloved in the life-drama.

One eventually moves on to the Rung of Community, where the harmonious collectivity of all souls is the highest concern. Having enjoyed the levels of creativity in the previous stages, we question whether this creativity is in itself of any benefit to others:

> Does the Earth get healed by it? Do exiles get released through it? Is the pool of knowledge enhanced by it? Are those people who need to work and dream and share together, working, dreaming and sharing together?

But this level of integration cannot occur until one has had the experience of the various games and names and roles of self and God within the Rung of Beauty.

By God's grace, we are then called to the Rung of Union. Union is an achievement that is beyond our efforts, and is of a reality that is, beyond our usual considerations, already present. That is to say, where the very identity of the soul with the Beloved, of God with the person, is already a fact. The realization of Union is what occurs on this rung, not the unchanging existence of Union. Periodic reflection on this truth is spiritual medicine for depression at any stage of practice.

In our daily meditations, we pray to the Divine who fills the world, and fills our hearts, and moves us from rung-to-rung, until we arrive at where we have always been. And then we take another step so that the soul can come to encompass the vastness of the knowable as well as the unknowable.

ON THE MEANING OF 'MYSTICAL'

If we were to make a distinction between the mystical and dogmatic elements in religious practice, the distinction would boil down to how much of the experiential element is present. Mystical doctrine claims that we can experience the Infinite right now, that beneath the surface of the obvious, there exists Divinity.

The dogmatic approach, on the other hand, doubts the possibility of experiencing God on this plane, and contents itself with belief in revealed principles, reasoned theology, outward observances and ritual. Religious dogmatists see little purpose in looking below the surface for hidden meanings and experiences. Religious mystics, on the other hand, see little purpose in simply reciting prayer formulae and not looking beyond them.

People seem naturally drawn to one of these two positions: to the exoteric, focusing on outer behavior and ritual practice, or to the esoteric search for the inner experience.

In the Jewish tradition, the mystical body of knowledge is called *kabbalah*, which literally means, 'that which is received.' Kabbalah is transmitted orally, only the outlines being written down. This is in part to protect it from being used without guidance, and because the mystical experience doesn't translate very well from direct experience into indirect words.

There is a teaching in Kabbalah that tells of the original 'vessels' created by God "in the beginning," which God filled to the brim with Divine Light. The full force of God's

Light was too much for these vessels and they shattered, showering shards of vessel and sparks of light everywhere. Eventually, shells formed on the outside of these sparks of light, hiding the sparks within them; this is the basis of the material world we live in today.

The Hasidic masters taught that these sparks of divinity reside in everything, animate and inanimate, and that each of us has it in our power to redeem the imprisoned sparks and send them back up to their divine Source, to rejoin Divinity. The Kabbalah teaches that this release and reunion of sparks is accomplished by every holy act.

What defines such an act is not only the outer prescriptions of behavior in the Jewish tradition, but also what we are doing on the inner plane. When we are offering the outer act of love, obedience and service, that is only the shell of it. On the inner level, we are sorting out sparks, offering them up, creating a *tikkun*, a 'fix' or 'rectification' for the original catastrophe of the shattering.

That, at least, is the classical formulation. From another point of view, there was never a catastrophe; only a loving, intentional, and creative act. The fact that things are not totally symmetrical creates the possibility, the im-balance that allows for this particular reality. The 'fall' from the Garden of Eden, then, was not a fall at all; it was a 'set-up' to allow the human being to individuate, to become a self-conscious, individual being.

LEVELS OF THE SOUL

Our discussion of the stages of practice and the meaning of mysticism must be combined with an understanding (and experience) of the levels of the soul. The lowest of the five levels, according to the Kabbalah, is called *nefesh* and corresponds to the aspect of action. The other levels, in ascending order, are *ru'ah*, *neshamah*, *hayyah* and *yehidah*. *Ru'ah* is the feeling level, and *neshamah* is the intellective. *Hayyah* and *yehidah* are beyond the verbal and discursive mind, but may be considered, respectively, as the levels of life beyond our understanding and the primary monad of self in eternal Union with God. The Zohar says, "Each is given a *nefesh*. If one so merits (by refining oneself), one is granted *ru'ah*, etc." So we start out with *nefesh*, and refine the soul from there through each of the other four levels by means of intention and meditation.

Let's look at these levels with an analogy. Assume I'm looking at a person and asking myself questions about their character, who they are, how it is that I know them. At this level, I can say I know the person because of the body they inhabit, what it looks like, what its habits are of cleanliness, of dress, of behavior. This is the level of *guf*, of body.

Nefesh

But this does not tell the whole story, of course. There is energy present and flowing in a handshake, for example, where I feel that I am in contact with that part of the person that is more than the person's physical body, that partakes, in addition, of the person's unique energy-field. This is the level of *nefesh*, where Nature fills us with energy and vitality, just as She fills all creatures and creation.

Ki ha'dam hu ha'nefesh, "for the blood is the life." (Deut. 12:23) The pulse, breath and skin-tone are *nefesh*, and all these are an expression of the vital principle in the person. *Nefesh* is a word that is associated with out-breath. It is written, "On the seventh day God rested." (Gen. 2:2) God expired, exhaled that breath that is *nofesh*, 'the out-breath' that is relaxation. After the in-breath necessary to do the work comes the letting go of the out-breath. In this letting go we rest in that primordial energy-pool in the body, the energy-pool that is shared, not only with other human beings, but also with plants and perhaps even 'lower' orders of being. Wherever there is desire, movement or vital-energy, we speak of the presence of *nefesh*.

Nefesh can be cultivated and activated as a potent force within us; but it must be aroused first. This we can do with meditation exercises that shift primary identity from the body, from *guf* to *nefesh*. This is to be coupled with the active observance of the appropriate *mitzvot*, or 'commandments'—because *nefesh* asserts itself as the 'self' in active fulfillment.

Nefesh-craft is manifested in the martial arts, in Hatha Yoga and T'ai Chi, and also in the fervor of our swaying in *davvenen*, in intimate prayer.

Ru'ah

Within this field of energy, there is attitude, posture and direction, bringing qualities of mood and intention that are beyond vitality. This is a manifestation of *ru'ah*. In a lilac bush, for example, there is *rayah*, 'fragrance.' The lilac says: "I am beautiful; behold me. Come, insects, draw from me my pollen for Nature's work." That is the animating power of vitality with direction. More than just propagation, it suggests growth and going beyond the boundaries of 'self.'

Ru'ah is not only found in the plant kingdom, of course; it is also found in animals and human beings. There is also a level on which we speak of angels as being *ruhot*. *Osseh malakhav ruhot, meshar'tav esh lohet*, "God makes angels," literally 'messengers,' "*ruhot*," or *ru'ah*-beings. (Ps. 104:4).

Ru'ah means, 'spirited,' a presence inhabiting space. So special places, holy places, will also have a *ru'ah* of their own. The artistry of *ru'ah* shows in good drama, in soulful music, in devout adoration, and can be felt in a stirring *niggun*, or wordless melody.

Neshamah

We have spoken of *nefesh* as the out-breath of relaxation, while *ru'ah* can be considered the breath held in anticipation and deep intent. In this analogy, *neshamah* is the in-breath. The word itself, *neshima*, is related to the Hebrew word for breathing-in, or derivatively, for being breathed *into*, that is to say, *inspired*.

It is written, "And God breathed the breath of life into the earthling's nostrils, and Adam became a living being." (Gen. 2:7) The Targum gives us a translation that says that Adam became *ru'ah memallela*, a 'speaking being.' This implies the entirety of our ability to have thoughts and to express them, to direct thoughts and share them, to hold thoughts and see the vastnesses in them. It is in thought that we construct and discover our maps of reality, and *neshamah* is that which, uniquely human, is ever involved in this process. While sensitive to contexts, it abstracts from discrete facts to the fields, theories and visions it apprehends.

Hayyah

Nefesh we know by feeling it with our senses. *Ru'ah* we know by affect, emotionally. *Neshamah* we can know through thought, through reason. Beyond this, the soul is not directly describable in words. How can I describe the quality I see in color, or that which I feel in warmth? Though it isn't essentially a verbal matter, ordinarily, all I have to communicate it is a verbal symbol, a collusion between people to agree on what we mean by 'color' or 'warmth.' But on the basic level of direct experience, its *is-ness* is non-verbal.

While there are non-verbal elements in sensation and feeling, in the realm of reason, we operate with words. But when we go beyond reason to the essential longing and yearning of the spark for the flame, there is *hayyah*, where living is its own 'truth.' *Hayyah*, as the name implies, is the life-element, the will-element, the will to live. It is the life-force that cannot be turned into an object.

Yehidah

Beyond the program to live is the realm of intuition, a knowledge of the Self by the self that happens in *yehidah*. It is essentially identical with the Divine, and as the name suggests, is the primary monad. When we speak about *Helek Eloha mi'ma'al mammash*, we speak of an absolute part of the Absolute, a singularly unique holographic particle of God. It is clear that there is no distance, no abyss dividing *yehidah* from the *yahid*, the One Infinite Being.

REFLECTION:

On Human Identity

WHEN WE SPEAK about a person, we mean the concatenation of body and these five orders of soul. As the attunement and attention vary from level to level, or where we focus at a particular time, that is the part of the soul that is then manifest. If I am involved in athletics, I'm most likely attuned to *nefesh*, and my *nefesh* is in an active state. If I listen to a piece of music, or attend a drama, then my *ru'ah* is most likely involved, while my *nefesh* is in a quiescent state. When meditating on ideas, I'm attuned primarily to *neshamah*, and not to other parts of my being.

Now, though we speak of these levels distinctly, they are of course inter-dependent. This is what we mean by the phenomenon of the *Merkavah*, or 'chariot,' so often spoken of in Kabbalah. Even while I'm in meditation, or contemplating with *neshamah*, I need the assistance of

---

ru'ah and *nefesh,* as well as the body. So my *neshamah* is riding in the *ru'ach* of an awakened heart, which is riding in the *nefesh* of an awakened energy-field, which is riding on the *guf* of an awakened body. In this kind of chariot, one vehicle is invested in another.

Further, I cannot say that the rider in the chariot is the *neshamah,* because even it is being driven by something that rides higher, the *hayyah.* And *hayyah* itself is being energized and focalized into existence by the specificity of that *yehidah,* which is the individuated aspect of the Infinite.

Here is an example that illustrates the dynamic interplay of the levels of soul:

> There is a compliment that nobody has given me before, but that I feel I deeply deserve. Of all the compliments I've ever received, all of them are chaff in comparison to this one I have not yet received. It is the important one. Then somebody gives me this compliment and I begin to cry. Why am I crying? What has happened?

What has happened is not just that affect has felt pleasure in the compliment, but that *hayyah,* that part of myself for which I do the deepest things in my life, has suddenly found recognition of its intention and let go. The melting that takes place at such a moment is *hayyah* melting through the dimension of ru'ah, and the purpose of my life is given a moment of fulfillment. All the trouble it has taken to get here seems to have been rewarded. It was worth it.

That peak experience affirming that "it was worth it," is what's called, *Olamekha tir'eh b'hayyekha.* This is getting *Olam ha'Ba,* the 'world-to-come,' in this world; and the striving is over at that moment. There is a sense of 'I'm home.' That excites *yehidah.* And if we can stay with this

> in the heart, not 'clinging' to it, but staying with it and breathing into it further, suddenly we see it not from the point of view of the recipient, but from the point of view of the Divine Grantor. And my identity is for that moment with the Divine, saying, "My child, today I have begotten you; this was the purpose of eternity."
>
> ∞

THE FOUR WORLDS

A PERSON CAN EXPERIENCE the inner process of deep prayer or redemptive action on four levels, which the Kabbalah calls the *arba olamot,* or 'four worlds.' Each of these worlds expresses a different way of experiencing God, each with unique laws and potentialities. In ascending order, these are: *Assiyah*, the world of doing; *Yetzirah*, the world of feeling; *Be'riyah*, the world of knowing; and *Atzilut*, the world of being.

Within Jewish mysticism, these inner-spaces are represented by the letters of the Divine Name, *Y-H-V-H:* the *Yud* representing *Atzilut*; the *Heh* representing *Be'riyah*; the *Vav* representing *Yetzirah*; and the lower *Heh* representing *Assiyah*. When these letters are stacked one on top of the other like the worlds (instead of side-by-side), they look like the figure of a human being. This suggests that we are made in the image of God.

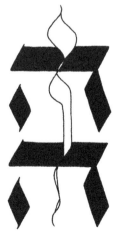

Assiyah

Assiyah, or 'doing,' is the designation for the physical world of action, which includes action for spiritual purposes. It is the world of the *guf* and *nefesh*, the body and its energies, located in the realm of sensation and behavior. The Jewish code of religious practice, the *halakhah*, operates largely in *Assiyah*. On this level, religion trains people in behaviors intended to please God by obedience to the divine law, and piety is expressed mostly through *g'millut hassadim*, doing 'deeds of loving-kindness' and observing the *mitzvot*.

Yetzirah

The inner experience of feeling or deep emotion is in the world of *Yetzirah*, where we find *ru'ah*, the 'breath-spirit.' *Yetzirah*, which means 'formation,' also involves images, values and myths. On this level, piety is measured in terms of devoutness: the sincere feeling one invests in prayer and worship. Purification of emotions is one of the central tasks to be accomplished on this level, and is a prerequisite for full entry into the world of the Kabbalah.

Be'riyah

The third level of reality is the world of *Be'riyah*, or 'creation,' the world of thinking and philosophy, thought or contemplation, where we seek to understand the blueprint of the universe. This is where the *neshamah* is rooted. *Be'riyah* also includes the faculties of concept, idea, hypothesis and theory. On this level, piety expresses itself in how one invests time and awareness in the study of Torah and the esoteric teachings.

Atzilut

The fourth level of reality is *Atzilut*, or 'emanation.' This is the world of being, intuition, inner teaching, the 'secret' and 'mystery' of *sod*, and the anagogical level of interpretation. *Atzilut* is a deep, Divine intuition—a state of 'beingness' with God in the soul's aspects of *hayyah* and *yehidah (yehidah,* actually, is what is 'touching' *Adam Kadmon).* It is the source of inspiration, the place where we speak of God as a person, clothing the divine in a 'root metaphor,' an archetypal image, like father, mother, sovereign, healer, beloved, and friend. These images put us on the soul level of *hayyah,* creating a covenantal relationship with the divine.

These worlds do not refer to the physical cosmology of planets and such (though these are included), but rather, describe a ladder of intersecting reality-patterns through which we (and all the Universe) ascend and descend, physically and spiritually. They also relate to the process of daily prayer, which, in our *siddur* or 'prayer-book,' is arranged as a journey up through these worlds and down again.

INTRODUCTION TO JEWISH MEDITATION & CONTEMPLATION

FOR THOSE WHO ARE just beginning meditation practice, two of the most common difficulties are remaining focused and interested, and experiencing annoyance from various distractions. You will quickly find that there are in fact many 'outer' distractions—sights, sounds, and other sense impressions—that want to claim your attention. You can look for a quiet spot, find a comfortable chair and close your eyes; but having done this, your troubles only begin anew with an onrush of thoughts and inner sensations. Before your closed eyes, a host of images present themselves. You hear your breath and sense your heartbeat. You remember all sorts of things that have to be done. You feel all sorts of itches and twitches. It is difficult to settle the mind. At a later stage, you can consider certain aspects of these distractions; but, for now, try to look beyond these distractions to the kind of meditation you want to practice.

HASHKATAH

The practice most associated with meditation today is that of 'stilling the mind,' or *hashkatah* in Hebrew. On this subject, we are fortunate to have a description of just such a practice given by the Piasetzno Rebbe, Rabbi Kalonymos Kalmish Shapiro to his Hasid, Reb Elazar Bein. The following is taken from Reb Elazar's personal journal:

MEDITATION:
Stilling the Mind

B"H Concerning the matter of the new teaching dealing with the quieting of the mind, as taught by our holy *rebbe*, of blessed memory, the master began with the statement:

"A dream is a 60th part of a prophecy" . . . When we are asleep, and the mind and thought processes are stilled, the flow from above comes to infuse us, since we are not then relating to our usual pre-occupations . . . This is the sense in which "a dream is a 60th part of prophecy."*

Furthermore, one is more deeply aroused in prayer than in the study of the Torah. In the study of Torah, one is more engaged in one's own thinking process—I analyze,

---

* Be'rakhot 57b.

I think. But, in prayer, it is the opposite; one is engaged in dissolving one's self in it. . . . Thoughts and desires usually clamor in a person without ceasing . . . they connect and associate one with the other, and it is difficult for a person to keep from identifying with them.

He then gave us practical advice on how to calm the thoughts: . . . One should look at one's thoughts for a small amount of time—say a few minutes—and then begin to see how slowly the mind is emptying, and how the thoughts stop rushing in their usual manner. Then, one should begin to say a phrase, such as *Ribbono Shel Olam,* in order to connect the now empty mind with one thought of holiness. Then, one can begin to request in prayer what is needed, or in which way one needs to be made whole, or strengthened—as in faith, or in love.

He then said, and I quote his holy words: "I believe with perfect faith that You, the Most High, are the only One in Existence, the only One in the Universe, and that besides You, there is no other being except You, *Oybershter* (Most High)! And the entire Universe, and all that it contains, is nothing but the effulgence of You, *Y-H-V-H.*"

He repeated this a few times, but warned us not to pronounce this with so many words, nor with intensity. The whole point is to calm one's thoughts, and with intense proclaiming, one only arouses one's selfishness. So one is to state this affirmation very gently. . . .

He also said that one can utilize this stilling of the mind for the correction of all the lower modes of being; but not in terms of negations—only by affirming the good quality to which one wishes to convert the bad one. For instance, the person who wishes to overcome laziness, let them not affirm the need for the removal of laziness; but affirm their eagerness and their zeal.

> It is also possible to achieve the stilling of the mind by making use of a watch, looking at it for some time; this too will calm the flow of constant wanting, and the rushing of the mind. Then, when the mind is calm, that brings about the indwelling from Above. This will also help much to firm-up one's faith.
>
> After a few weeks of utilizing the stilling, when one says, "This is my God, and I will beautify Him,"* it becomes like pointing one's finger at the Creator.**
>
> ∞

Hitbonenut

ANOTHER SUBTLE and powerful technique of meditation or contemplation is called *hitbonenut,* or 'self-understanding.' It is a technique which comes from the Habad school of Hasidism, and which can be done in the course of one's daily prayers or separate from them. In it, one thoroughly explores a spiritual concept, filling one's awareness with it until it brings about a change in one's life.

At first, we think about the idea or concept in an objective way, attempting to understand it intellectually, down to its very last detail. But when we have finished filling-out the concept, and have mastered the thought-sequence in all its rich detail, we should then move into the dimension of situational-thinking. That is to say, we must re-invest the conceptual material with a 'real-life' context.

This situational mode of thought is called *ada'ata*

---

* Rashi's interpretation of Exodus 15:4.
** Rabbi Kalonymos Kalmish Shapiro was murdered in the Trawniki work camp near Lublin in 1943. Reb Elazar Bein fortunately escaped Europe in 1939 and made his way to Israel, where Rabbi Nehemia Polen met him and made a copy of his journal, thus preserving this teaching for us.

d'nafshei, 'soul-knowledge,' in the Jewish tradition, and fills us with an immediate emotional awareness that provokes us to action. For example, we might understand what it means in general for someone to inherit a large sum of money, considering the situation and all its various ramifications, such as the personal, social, and societal effects of a sudden acquisition of capital. But now imagine *you* are the *actual* beneficiary, right now, in this moment, *ada'ata d'nafshei*, finding yourself filled with emotion that begets a corresponding response in behavior. From this, you can immediately see just how vital *ada'ata d'nafshei* thinking can be to your meditation.

M'malleh Kol Almin

A traditional topic of *hitbonenut* is the Divine Indwelling in Creation. This idea is spoken of as *m'malleh kol almin*, God's 'filling all worlds' with light and life.

People often have a notion of there being a God 'out there,' 'somewhere' in the universe. And it is possible to construct a conceptual framework within which one might think about God in this way. But, as Reb Shneur Zalman of Liadi says in his *Likkutei Torah—Le'it mahshava te'fisa bah klal,* "There is no thought that can take hold of You." Thus, in time, we find ourselves at a loss, trying to think about God, and yet, knowing the futility of such an approach. Nevertheless, Reb Shneur Zalman continues, *aval nit'fas i'hu be're'uta de'liba,* "but the Infinite God is taken hold of by the longing of the heart." The longing of the heart is something that is not reaching toward an *idea*, but toward a *Presence* and a *Being*.

You see, when the "longing of the heart" takes over, we are no longer dealing with the God-idea in the third person; we are dealing with the second-person Presence of the living God. Here, I find myself alive in the Divine *milieu*. I am not talking about God, I am speaking to . . .

> You, O Life, O God, O Knower, O Beloved. I know that I am shaped and created by Your Love, and the very words that are rising in my mouth, and the feelings rising in my heart, are not my creation, but are made, focused, fielded, and made possible by You!

So we meditate on God 'filling our universe' with life, and we do this *ada'ata d'nafshei*. We are now, here, filled with Life, with God. We wonder at our own being, at our own body; this amazing biological factory, converting oxygen and food into consciousness and life. Our pulse is beating and our vitality fills us with curiosity. You see, reveling in this field that is not held together by our volition but by the grace of God holding us in life, is a way of getting to know God as immanent in creation.

But we, in our 'little selves,' are only tiny parts of this great universe, *v'olamot ain mispar*, "the worlds without number" (Song 6:8). There are worlds that are so short-lived, like muons and pions, fractions, millionths of a second, and worlds that are so vast that our galaxy itself pales beside them. Thus, we can begin to see the vastnesses of these vibrations in which a whole life can happen in a millionth of a second, or so slowly that one circuit of the Sun takes 226 million years! Each of these is 'filled' by God. So, when I speak of God, and think only of the vast and expansive God, I sometimes fail to recognize God in the infinitesimal life of a muon. We must remember that Divinity fills all creation, great and small!

When we face this tremendous fact, we feel something in our hearts; but that feeling is not as important as *Whom* we feel. When we reach this point in our meditation, we must hold on to it. In this, we face and behold God. As the emotion subsides, the subtlety of the meditation deepens, and form gives way to formlessness. It is at this stage that we allow the Divine in without reserve, and allow its power to re-orient our souls.

MEDITATION:

God 'Filling All Worlds'

EVERYTHING IS FILLED WITH LIFE. Wherever we turn, life abounds. The All vibrates in Song. Every individual cell is filled with life, as is every atom. All of life proceeds from a Source. "For with You is the source of Life, in Your Light we see Light" (Ps. 36:9). Life makes things live.

The Life is hidden in the things It invigorates. It cannot show Itself to them, lest they cease functioning as living beings. To faint is to be overwhelmed by one's life. If one's life leaves, one cannot live. Thus, Life must hide Itself in the very thing to which it gives life.

All of life is in continuous motion, moving to and fro, vibrating in harmony. Life is the effulgence of the Infinite. Like sunlight proceeding from the Sun, without effort on the part of the Sun, so does the Light of the Infinite proceed to reflect God. Everything alive basks in God's Radiance.

We are now being filled like a pitcher plunged in the sea, filled with water on the inside and surrounded by oceans of water without. In all our functions (every one of them pictured in detail), we are being filled with Life. Even in times of life-denial, we are still filled with this Life, which brings us to feel remorse. But we shouldn't turn fully in this direction at this moment. Rather, we visualize ourselves being filled by God, and all the worlds (from the highest to this, the lowest) being filled by God.

We also visualize God in our work and recognize that God fills our day, the vehicles we drive, the rooms we are

---

inhabiting, in the very places we are standing or sitting.

All this Life that surrounds us, challenges us to fulfill its wish to be reflected back to God. The very sidewalk says to us: "Cleave to God, to God's Torah and *mitzvot*, or else with what right do you step on me?!" The food we eat, (so full of life) also wishes to be reflected back to God. It, and every desirable and enjoyable thing, says to us: "Reflect me back to God! Do not see in me only an end, but rather as a means to express God as God fills me and surrounds me."

Now we say to ourselves, "God is always near me, nearer than the feeling I now feel." This beholding of Life filling the All bestows great joy. There is no despair, no loneliness, for God is always in us and in all things.

∞

Soveiv Kol Almin

Though God is inherent in all the light and life that clothes itself in creation, there is also another level of Divine Light where creation does not matter. Over and beyond that which can be caught and assimilated by creation, there is a Light surrounding, suffusing and permeating the worlds. This Light bathes the All. Neither high nor low, nor light nor dark, nor any of the bipolar concepts have room there. Good and evil are of no consequence here. This realm of God, existing in the *now*, is timeless. To It, there is no 'now,' no 'once,' no 'will be' in existence. Concerning this realm, we always say in our prayer-book, "You are the One who was before the creation of the world; You are the same after the creation of the world."

This is spoken of in Kabbalah as *soveiv kol almin*, God's light 'surrounding all worlds,' and it, like *m'malleh kol almin*, is another major subject of *hitbonenut* contemplation.

Concerning this transcendental realm, you might consider the following from the *Tanya (Sefer Shel Beinonim,* chapter 36) of Reb Shneur Zalman of Liadi:

> It cannot be said that for God there is either an up or down; for God fills all these worlds equally. Before the world was created, God and God's Name were One, filling all space in which the universes were created. And for God, there has been no change.

And this from the *Tanya (Sha'ar ha'Yihud ve'ha'Emunah,* chapter 7):

> There has been no change in God. Exactly as God was Alone before the creation of the world, so God is Alone after its creation. As we say, "You were God before the creation of the world; You have been God since the creation of the world." There has been no change either in God's Essence or in God's Knowledge, for God's Knowledge is merely Self-Knowledge, and God knows all creatures introspectively, for all is from God, and nullified within God.

> As Maimonides expressed it: "God is the Knower, the thing Known and Knowledge itself. This is a thing which is in the power of no mouth to utter, or in the power of no ear to hear, nor is it possible for the heart of any to grasp its full significance."* God, God's Essence, and God's Knowledge are absolutely One, from every single angle or viewpoint, in every possible type or identity. God's Knowledge is not something added to God's Essence, as in the case of the human being, whose knowledge is added to and grafted on to the self.

---

* Hilkhot Yesodei Ha'Torah, Chapter 2, Halakhah 10.

In the case of a human being studying something, intelligence precedes learning, and after study, the object of study is added to intelligence; and so, day-by-day, and year-by-year, by the continuance of this process, one becomes wise. But in the human being, the union of intelligence and knowledge is not a simple, but a compound unity.

However, the blessed and Holy One, is a simple Unity, without plurality of composition of any sort. Therefore, just as it is impossible for any creature in the world to conceive of God's Essence, so it is impossible to understand the nature of God's Knowledge. We can but believe with a faith which is above reason and conception that the blessed and Holy One, Who is Uniquely One, is identical with the Divine Knowledge.

By knowing God-self, God discerns and knows all the creatures, above and below, even down to the smallest fish in the sea and the tiniest insect in the bowels of the earth. Nothing is hidden from God. All this knowledge does not add to the Essence of the Holy One, or make God composite, since in knowing these things, God but knows God-self, and God's Essence and Knowledge are one and the same.

Because this is so difficult to imagine, the prophet has said: "For my thoughts are not your thoughts, and your ways are not my ways, says our Sustainer. For as high as the heavens are above the earth, so high are my ways above your ways, and my thoughts above your thoughts." (Isa. 55:8-9) And concerning this it is said: "Can you find out the experience of God? Or can you find [the way] unto the utmost limits of the Almighty?" (Job 11:7) And this was Job's question: "Have You eyes of flesh, or will You see as a mortal sees?" (10:4) For the human being sees and knows all things with a knowledge which is external to the self; but the blessed and Holy One knows all from a knowledge of God's Own Self.

Now, these are very important concepts in Habad Hasidism, and worth exploring further; but you should also feel free to branch-out, exploring other spiritual ideas in the same way, *ada'ata d'nafshei*, experiencing them personally and allowing them to transform you from the inside out.

Moreover, this practice takes deepening and repeating, over and over again. When I was a young man in the *yeshivah*, my *mashpiyya*, my spiritual mentor, would insist, "Repeat, repeat, repeat." The Hasidic master, Reb Pinhas of Koretz, put it this way: "The soul is an indifferent teacher . . . It doesn't repeat anything twice."[*] Therefore, we have to help the soul by ruminating on the experience, repeating the sequence over and over again. Remember, soul-craft calls for diligent, careful and caring work in the garden of mind.

KAVVANAH

IF WE ARE ABLE TO MEDITATE on God's immanence, as we have described, then God's indwelling becomes the essential component of our mental-functional life. To expand this practice from the mental domain to include our whole being, we practice with our whole being in the Presence of God. This discipline is the mainstay of spiritual life.

---

* See Zalman Schachter-Shalomi and Netanel Miles-Yépez, *A Heart Afire: Stories and Teachings of the Early Hasidic Masters*, Philadephia: Jewish Publication Society, 2009: 143, and note 30 on 353.

Kavvanah means 'intention,' the intention that is always free in us. Even if the whole world coerces us into a particular action, we can always 'intend' as we wish. In our day-to-day endeavors, for example, we do whatever we must do, while intending according to our understanding: "God of Law and Order, You have ordained work for human beings. In doing, I intend to do Your will. I wish to bind myself to You in this action, which is my offering to You."

Especially when doing a *mitzvah*, we should concentrate carefully on our intention. On *Shabbat*, for instance, when eating, we can intend, *Lih'vod ha'Shabbat*, 'honoring the Sabbath' . . . "May I eat this food and enjoy it for Your sake, for this is the *mitzvah* of the *Shabbat*." When putting on the *te'fillin*, or lighting the candles, we can intend: "Loving Sustainer, use my body as an instrument of Your Will. My limbs are prepared, and at Your disposal!" Then we say the blessing.

When I wrap myself in the *tallit*, I can do so with the *kavvanah* that, just as I wrap my body, so my soul is wrapped in the Divine Light. When I count the *Omer* between Pesah and Shavu'ot, each of the 49 days can be counted with the unique *kavvanah* that corresponds to the *se'firah* the Kabbalah associates with that day.*

Even if we are sitting in the dentist's chair, we can 'intend' our pain as an offering of love. Whether we are traveling far, or just doing our daily tasks, all our actions can be sanctified by offering them to God.

In prayer, our *kavvanah* is of vital importance. Of course, one can pray with an attitude that says we are only praying in order to fulfill an obligation, to 'get it over with,' rushing through it as fast as possible. Or, we can be intent on 'contacting' God in our prayers, praying truly and deeply

---

* See Min Kantrowitz, *Counting the Omer: A Kabbalistic Meditation Guide*, Santa Fe, NM: Gaon Books, 2009.

with *kavvanah*, making each word and phrase into a conscious act of communion.

It is helpful to have a visual image in *kavvanah*. You can picture the Will of God flowing into your body and soul, becoming united with the limbs, organs, senses, brain and nerves, and moving—by God's Will—to execute each *mitzvah*. This should become very familiar and firmly established in habit.

One possibility for experimenting with *kavvanah* is Reb Ahrele Roth's (the founder of the Roth lineage of Hasidism) list of thirty-two *mitzvot* to be fulfilled with *kavvanah* in the heart, and with the mouth:

MEDITATION:

Thirty-Two Mitzvot of the Heart

My Creator!
May Your Name be praised:
With my mouth, mind and heart prepared,
I am ready to fulfill Your *mitzvot*.

You Who shape me:

1. Faith I place in You;
2. Oneness I affirm in You;
3. I am mindful of You;
4. I focus on Your vast greatness,
5. And on my own insignificance;
6. Thus do I turn back to You in *teshuvah*,
7. And am bashful in Your Presence;
8. I am awed by You,
9. And love You;

---

10. I accept the authority
of Your *mitzvot*,
11. Find my joy in You,
12. And place my trust in You;
13. I deny all false gods
And those in their service,
Rejecting all unfit thoughts
That arise in my heart;
14. I give You my thanks,
15. And aim to hold You sacred;
16. I remember Jerusalem,
Your House of Prayer
For all Peoples,
17. And look to You,
To redeem us
And free our souls;
18. Amalek, I will blot out,
19. By loving my neighbor as myself,
20. And adhering to You in *de'veikut*,
21. Walking in Your ways;
22. Thus, will I make in me a holy space
For You to be at home;
23. I long for Your intimacy and love,
24. And am energized to find You
Empowering my heart;
25. I affirm that Your actions are just,
26. And am mindful that You
Redeem us from *Mitzrayim*;
27. Therefore, I will not welcome,
In my awareness, any thought
That opposes faith in Your service,
And in Your Torah;
28. I will not yield to pride;
29. I will not hate any fellow
God-wrestler in my heart,

30. And I will give up all vindictiveness,
And not consider myself flawless,
31. But remember that I
Caused You displeasure;
32. With all these, I intend not
To forget Your Presence
In my life.
Amen!

Thus,
May You be pleased,
Celestial Parent,
That by the merit
And the power
Of my making mention
Of these *mitzvot*
With my mouth,
There be stimulated
The energy of these *mitzvot*
In their Celestial Root,
To draw down to me,
That high Holy Flow
That will shield my thoughts,
My voice and my words,
From all damage,
All taint, all dross and dirt.
And there be drawn to me
A flow that will make pure
My thoughts and heart,
My voice and words.
May all of them
Be surrendered
To You, be You praised,
To the end that I may merit
To be connected to You,
In *de'veikut* and love,

And to attain
The fulfillment
Of Your *mitzvah*
To cleave to You.

Thus will I be privileged
To be an instrument
Of Your Will,
A vehicle for the
Blessed *Shekhinah,*
Of Your Glory.

Thus,
Will the light
In my soul
Not darken,
Nor will Your
Divine spark
Be extinguished in me,
From now on
And forever.
Amen![*]

∞

DE'VEIKUT

THE HOLY BA'AL SHEM TOV, the founder of Hasidism, often spoke of a triad: *shiflut* (humility), *hitlahavut* (fervor), and *de'veikut* (clinging to God). *De'veikut* implies *dibbuk haverim*, the 'closeness of friends,' and *le'davka bo*, to 'stick together' with God. *De'veikut* is the inverse of *shiviti*, as in

---

[*] See Zalman Schachter-Shalomi and Yair Hillel Goelman, (ed. and trans.), *Ahron's Heart: The Prayers, Teachings and Letters of Ahrele Roth, A Hasidic Reformer,* Teaneck, NJ: Ben Yehuda Press, 2009: 41-69.

Shiviti Ha'Shem le'negdi tamid, "I place *Y-H-V-H* before me always" (Ps. 16:8), to see all of reality as Divine. So clinging is 'inside,' and seeing God before me is 'outside.'

The word *de'veikut* is from the root *D-B-K*, which means 'glue,' or 'being in touch.' The antonym of *D-B-K* is derived from *P-R-D/T,* meaning 'aPaRT,' or 'sePaRaTe,' as when one speaks of being *niFRaD*, or 'cut-off' in Hasidism. To illustrate the shift in attitude from *nifrad* to *de'veikut*, let us notice that when we are engaged in pursuing something, intent only on our own purpose, in that moment, we experience ourselves as *nifrad*. It is only a simple shift in *kavvanah* that changes our purpose to engage in the same action while cleaving to God in *de'veikut*. And it is that recognition which we see in that wonderful verse, *Akhein attah Eyl Mistater,* "So here You are, hidden God" (Isa. 45:15) I am aware that I am in You, and You are in me, and we are not really separable. Then, *de'veikut* is not something that I have to make; *de'veikut* is something that I have to discover. It is not a natural state to be *nifrad*. The natural state is to be in *de'veikut*. The practice of *de'veikut* is to affirm that a state of grace, of non-duality—'not-two'—is always present.

Since *de'veikut* is close to the unitive, but not identical with it, it may be said that it corresponds to the relationship of light with the lumen, the self-effulgent source of light. This also implies a sense of *bittul*, or 'effacement' of the one who is in *de'veikut*. It is rather a joyous willingness to be transparent, to be the vehicle for the light. Here resides a deep bliss with tinges of awesomeness.

MEDITATION:

Various Kinds of De'veikut

1. As we touch a *mezuzah* on entering
Or exiting a dwelling, we remember God.

2. When someone calls,
Or before we speak to someone,
We imagine that God is listening-in.

3. When we need a short rest,
As we settle into it, we visualize
God's everlasting arms receiving us.

4. We wash dishes and feel
The Divine Presence in our hands,
In the water, and in the dishes.

5. We eat, and as we taste the food,
We offer the pleasure of our palate to God.

6. In a moment of difficulty, we exhale
With a prayer, and receive a response
With the in-breath.

7. We talk with another
And affirm in our heart that
The Beloved is in us both.

Though there are many insights available in this state, we haven't any interest in gathering them, as we are busy 'being one.' We may then bring the *de'veikut* to the place in ourselves we find in need.

Once, I composed a chant that goes like this:

It is perfect;
You are loved;

> All is clear,
> And I am holy.
>
> "It is perfect," is *de'veikut* in the world of *Assiyah*. "You are loved," is *de'veikut* in *Yetzirah*. "All is clear" is *de'veikut* in *Be'riyah;* and "I am holy" is *de'veikut* in *Atzilut.*
>
> These are all moments of unique recognition. In these exercises, we see how *de'veikut* is a form of practicing the Presence of God, seeing God's immanence in all creation.
>
> ∞

SHIVITI

THE *SHIVITI* IS A CHART FOR GAZING, composed of the four letters of the Divine Name, *Y-H-V-H*, as well as additional mystical formulae. In gazing at the *shiviti*, we allow ourselves to enter into its power, and to be filled with its illumination.

For example, one way in which the four-letter-name of God can be read is as *Yud HoVeH*. *Yud* is a 'point,' and *hoveh* is the 'present'—that very point in the present. The *shiviti* reminds us of this radical present, that we're right here, that we don't have to create the past, nor the future. We're right at this *ne'kudot hoveh*, this 'point in the present.'

In the *shivui*, the equanimity of this situation, we realize that we are not deprived of anything. We realize that even the inner programming for life that keeps us going is not really necessary at this moment, and we are ready to let go of that attachment. In the world of the intellect, where our 'reality-map' is located, we are likewise obliged to let go of formulation. For in the *shiviti*, every possibility, every cosmology is possible. If we are ready for the truth of this moment, an entire cosmology opens up before us that fits this moment. It further suggests the contingency of all our favorite reality-maps, the assumed common law of shared experience.

As other traditions have developed particular techniques of using the gaze in spiritual practice—such as with mandalas and icon gazing—so *shiviti*, name gazing, is a basic Jewish tool for spiritual work. As in the practices of other traditions, the goal of *shiviti* is to move from the outside to the inside, so that we become one with the Divine:

MEDITATION:
The Glowing Letters of the Name

ONE EXAMPLE of the joint practice of *shiviti* and *de'veikut* is suggested by the great mystic, Rabbi Hayyim Vital. In this exercise, we close our eyes and visualize the Holy Name, *Y-H-V-H*, noticing which letter 'glows' most intensely for us. If the *Yud* is the one most charged, one might put intuition at the disposal of *de'veikut*. If the first or upper *Heh* is most charged, then it is the mind that is put at the disposal of *de'veikut*. If the *Vav*, then the feelings are given over to *de'veikut*. And if it is the final or lower *Heh* that is most charged, the body is put at the disposal of *de'veikut*.

∞

Looking at the *shiviti*, we view the world from God's vantage point. Thus, *hesed*, God's right hand, as it were, is not opposite to ours, as if we were looking in a mirror. It is on our right, as if we were standing just behind God. This is connected to what God says to Moses on Mount Sinai, "You shall see my back; my face is not to be seen." (Ex. 33:23) So one walks, as it were, into the *Y-H-V-H,* facing in the same direction, becoming one with it.

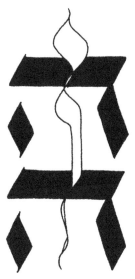

The Divine Name is written in such a way—top to bottom, rather than right to left—to create a hierarchy and also a human figure: *Yud* is the head; the upper *Heh*, the shoulders and arms; *Vav*, the heart, spine and genitals; and the lower *Heh*, the pelvis and legs.

These correspond to the four worlds and the *se'firot*, or divine attributes: the very tip or point at the top of the letter *Yud* is the attribute, *keter;* the rest of the letter *Yud* is the world of *Atzilut* and the attribute, *hokhmah;* the upper *Heh* is the world of *Be'riyah* and the attribute, *binah;* the letter *Vav* is the world of *Yetzirah* and contains the lower attributes, *hesed, gevurah, tiferet, netzah, hod* and *yesod;* and finally, the lower *Heh* is the world of *Assiyah* and the attribute, *malkhut.*

MEDITATION:
Breathing the Divine Name

IN THE KABBALAH, the phases of breath also correspond to the letters in the Divine Name. Visualizing the letters stacked one on top of the other, in a human form, try the following breathing meditation practice:

1. After an exhalation, when there is no breath left in your lungs, imagine the letter *Yud* of the Divine Name in the place of your head;

2. When you inhale and expand the lungs, imagine the upper *Heh* of the Divine Name in your shoulders and arms;

3. Now hold the breath in your lungs for a moment and imagine the letter *Vav* of the Divine Name in your spine;

4. Then when you exhale and deflate the lungs, imagine the lower *Heh* of the Divine Name in your pelvis and legs;

5. With the last exhalation complete, your lungs are empty and you imagine the letter *Yud* of the Divine Name in the place of your head again, and you continue this breathing pattern through several cycles.

This powerful practice gives us a rhythmic awareness of *Y-H-V-H* in our very body and breath. To do this breathing meditation, and to become aware of one's own inner Divinity, is a great blessing.*

∞

---

* Extrapolated from the teachings of the Spanish kabbalist, Rabbi Yosef ibn Gikatilla.

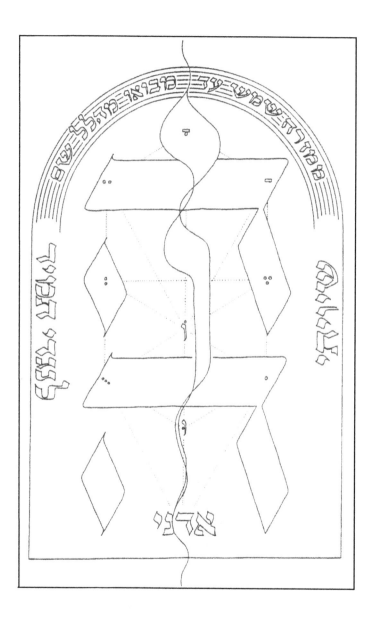

In prayer, one sits in front of the *shiviti* and stares at it to ascend to God's Presence, and then to descend. In this context, the four letters of the Divine Name represent the parts of the prayer service: in the morning prayer, one looks at the lower *Heh* during the *Birkhot ha'Shahar*, the opening blessings which address the world of *Assiyah*, the world of our bodies, our environment; getting ready in *Assiyah* requires doing an inventory of the body. For instance, asking questions life, 'What tensions are my muscles holding on to?' To place oneself in the presence of God is to let the body out from under any compulsion.

During the *Pe'sukei de'Zimra*, the prayers and psalms of thanksgiving, we turn our attention to the *Vav*, representing the world of *Yetzirah*, the world of feelings, emotions, and affect. Here, the grateful mentality reigns. We are thankful with humility, because we know that we are receiving love without having had to earn it. And we are equally thankful for the tribulations and pain we have suffered, which have enabled us to grow and learn.

With *Barkhu* and *Yotzeir Or*, we enter the world of intellect, *Be'riyah*, and our focus turns to the upper *Heh*. Here, we want to be open to any truth that wants to burst forth, without predilections. So we let go of our expectations that reality will turn out this way or that way. If we do that, then what will come to us will be precisely what this moment requires.

And finally, the goal of the *shiviti* is realized as we come to the world of *Atzilut*, or being, with the *Amidah*, the silent prayer. We look at the *Yud*, and the *shiviti*, which we initially placed opposite us, moves from the outside to the inside, through our skin, so that we become one with the Divine. The *shiviti* is no longer external, it burns within us. If your experience something of this, try to stay in this state as long as possible.

INTRODUCTION TO THE
LADDER OF TRADITIONAL PRAYER

THE PRAYER OF DOING — ASSIYAH

THERE IS NOT a very great difference between meditative practice and formal daily *davvenen*, or deep prayer. In each case, we prepare ourselves and our space for holy work with the appropriate intention. Thus, we preface our prayers with other prayers that ask that we be able to pray.

Then, in the opening section of the morning liturgy, we begin by focusing in our bodies. This is the section called *Birkhot ha'Shahar*, which deals with the movements that would replicate a conscious arising, clothing ourselves and preparing for worship.

We begin with a grateful mentality. If we fill the mind with gratitude, with astonishment, with delight, then this attunement is going to fill all our further actions. Such an attitude brings us to joyous arousal. We tune ourselves to be the sweet instrument on which God plays:

Thank You, Living God,
For mercifully granting
My soul another day
Of awareness;
Thank You for
This sacred trust.

Our bodies give us messages to which we are frequently deaf. But the physical sensations are only the vehicles of the message—the attention-getters. The messages sent by the body do not come in words; they come as a kind of feeling, a deep body-sense. When the body is clear, and in a state of well-being, we are able to focus the entire self—soul and body—in the present tense, in this very moment.

When basic needs are met, and appreciated whole-heartedly with awareness, it is easier for us to climb the spiritual ladder. If, however, we attempt to climb the ladder before reaching this condition of well-being, there will be problems. So the early part of our liturgy begins with attunement at this basic level.

Among our most primary functions is breathing, and in this section is the blessing for our breath: *Elohai neshamah she'natata bi, tehora hi,* "God, the soul You give me is pure." In Hebrew, the word for this aspect of soul means 'breathe,' and breathing exercises are well done in conjunction with it:

My God, the breath
You have given me
Is pure and refreshing;
You create it, *You* form it,
You breathe it into me,
And *You* keep me Breathing.

One day—
You will take
It from me;
I will have breathed
My last breath
In this body,
And *You* will
Resuscitate me

To the life of the spirit.

With every breath
Still in me,
I thank You, my God,
God of my forebears,
Sustenance of all spirits,
Master of all that happens.

I worship *You—Yah*,
Who with each breath,
Gives me life anew.

Awareness of our actual body experience is one of the most important keys to spiritual work. Windows to this awareness are built into the tradition. So when I begin in the morning and look at my body functions, one of the first functions I meet is elimination. After we go to the bathroom, there is blessing for the successful completion of this most elementary and necessary act, the *Asher Yatzar* blessing:

I worship You,
Yah, Our God,
Cosmic Majesty;
You formed me
A human being,
So wisely;
You created in me
All manner of
Hollows and ducts,
Inner organs
And intestines.

As I am completely
Transparent before You,

It is apparent and clear,
That if any of these
Openings would clog,
Or if any of these
Enclosures would seep,
I could not exist
And live in Your sight,
Not even for a moment.

So I'm grateful
And bless You
For healing me
In amazing ways.

The morning blessings continue: "Blessed are You, God, Sovereign of the Universe, who takes those who are bent and straightens them out . . . who opens the eyes of the blind . . . who gives me firm ground on which to stand . . . who girds me with strength." If we accompany these blessings with appropriate postures, our bodies serve to bring the blessings into sharp focus. Standing up, straightening up the body, bending down and straightening up again, feeling clothes on ourselves, we are surrounding our bodily functions with the blessings that are the attunement to the grateful mentality. Then, when we are finished with the first part of the service, the body is really present and willing to participate in prayer. As Rebbe Nahman of Bratzlav said, "Teach the body of all the delights of the soul so that the body will not be left behind."[*]

[*] *Likkutei Maharan I*, 22:5. See Zalman Schachter-Shalomi and Netanel Miles-Yépez, *A Hidden Light: Stories and Teachings of Early HaBaD and Bratzlav Hasidism*, Santa Fe, NM: Gaon Books, 2011: 294-98.

GUIDANCE:
Spirit and Flesh

REB NAHMAN TELLS US that from each Torah teaching we should make a prayer asking that the teaching become realized in our life. In the same way, each ecstatic soul-experience should be shared with the body. In this way, the body will also look forward to spiritual experiences and hold the attitude of being connected with the ecstasy. At such times, when due to the soul's ups and downs, one is no more connected with the bliss of the center, one may, by tuning-in with the body, get restored to joyous service. This makes it much more likely to pick-up the higher perspective again.

There is great subtlety in what the body can do for which we have no words; yet, caring attention to what the body is feeling, and watching for proprioceptive landmarks, can make them accessible to recall. Before prayer and before *Shabbat*, it is useful to spend some time recalling ecstatic body responses to soul-states. Thus, when bathing and dressing for *Shabbat*, if we can hum a *niggun,* or recite an appropriate holy phrase with the right celebrative *nussah,* the recalling becomes easier.

Each time we have a holy, ecstatic, or celebrative experience and say the blessing *Sheheheyanu,* we add this experience to the garland of holy moments. At any time, we are free to return to them, and, in the way of the body-memory, we can re-experience them and give thanks for them in a holy mini-vacation. Such grateful and holy mindfulness is itself a prayer and casts out a great deal of melancholy. When we manage to connect the general state of "Strength and joy are in God's peace" with the words *Barukh Ha'Shem* and *Barukh attah Ha'Shem,* we give the body a way to participate in our prayers and blessings.

Meanwhile, the phantom body is always free. Many athletes have learned that they can always be training, even when they are not in the gym. All they need to do is use the phantom body to exercise. So, even when one is in circumstances where it is not possible to use the physical body in prayer, one can still use the phantom body.

Do a slow motion genuflection as in the *Aleinu*—bowing to the right and to the left, and with a deep knee-bend toward the front—realizing all the tensings and flexings and relaxings of the muscles. Then, sitting in a contemplative position, repeat the movement with only the barest sub-muscular isometric movement and execute the whole outer movement on the inner plane—enriched by the imaginative addition of significances, feelings and actions. This will help you immensely in your *davvenen*. We can always visit our favorite house of God on the inner plane, while on the outer we remain in circumstances most fitting our sense of what lends the greatest harmony. In this way, we can dance in our seat, and kneel and prostrate before God.

∞

There are several orders for *Birkhot Ha'Shahar,* the blessings of the morning, and they are not exactly the same. There is an Ashkenazi (northern European) order, a Sefardi order (southern European and Mediterranean), and a *Nussah Ari* order, based on the teaching of the kabbalist, Rabbi Yitzhak Luria, called the Ari, or 'lion.' I prefer the *Nussah Ari* order because it best fits my understanding. The *Ari* begins with the awareness that the day is dawning, and the rooster is crowing. The next blessing is on opening the eyes, "Oh, I can see." The next one is, "I can stretch!" My limbs are free from the bonds of sleep. Then, "I stand up on firm ground and straighten." "I can walk—my steps have been prepared for me." "I have clothes"—*malbish arumim*. "I have everything I need"—*she'asah li kol tzor'ki*—even shoes.

The Holy Ari's version takes me first into the body, and then to higher functions which recognize that I am made in God's image, that I am made free, that I am made a 'God-wrestling' Israelite.* And after the God-wrestling, it says, *ha'notein laya'eif ko'ah*, 'who gives strength to the weary.'

When I hear that God "girds Israel with strength" there, I have the sense of feeling my own strength and power. It is not simply a raw brawn; it has a certain elegance—*oter Yisrael be'tifara*, "who crowns Israel with beauty"—it has an aesthetic quality. Then I come to the *B'rakhot* that are the 'blessings' of awareness and mind, and I end up giving thanks that sleep has passed from my eyes. I then prepare my mind for learning this day. So I say everything today is going to be a learning experience: *Barukh attah Ha'Shem . . . asher kid'shanu be'mitzvotav ve'tzivanu la'asok be'divrei Torah*, or *al divrei Torah*. 'Blessed are You . . . who connects us with holiness by commanding us to engross ourselves in the words of teaching.' So the whole world is a teacher, and I open myself to it.

We then come to the second part of the morning *davvenen*, or 'prayer,' where the Temple sacrifices are recounted. This section is called the *Korbannot*, and is focused on the plane of *Assiyah*, the place of spiritual action. This part of the service encourages us to begin exploring internal spiritual spaces, to make sure that there are coals burning on the inner altar.

The first part recounts how Abraham offers Isaac as a sacrifice. In this section, I learn that even the most beloved

---

* The Hebrew word, *Yisra'el* means, 'one who struggles,' or 'wrestles with God.'

possession that I have, I have to be willing to offer to God. Then, I offer myself in the little *Sh'ma'*, and then offer the world and what I own—whether sheep, or incense, or whatever. Today, the *Korbannot* sections dealing with the specific sacrifices offered in the Temple in Jerusalem are something that one might choose to omit, not because they aren't worthy of recounting, but because they are so distant from our current experience of the world. In any case, I keep returning to the basic meaning of sacrifice— that one who is offering a sacrifice to God must bring of themselves—*Adam ki yak'riv mikem korban Ha'Shem* (Lev. 1:2).

זַ וֹ וֹ

The Prayer of Feeling — Yetzirah

When the body is aroused, we can move on to the prayer of feeling in *Pe'sukei de'Zimra*, the 'hymns of praise,' corresponding to the world of *Yetzirah*, which deals with the attunement of affect, emotion and attitude. The primary activity here is praise—*halleluyah:* "Praise God, all the angels; Praise God, sun and moon and stars of light; Praise God, sea monsters and all the denizens of the sea, fish, birds, trees and beast, young men and maidens, old folks and little kids, kings and bureaucrats, all sing *halleluyah!*" (Ps. 148). The Psalms are the main component of this section of the service, providing abundant material to arouse one's feelings.

But notice the change in rhythm here. Affect moves with a slower, more organic speed, swelling and abating, pulsating blood and breath. It is clearly a different speed than that of the mind, which operates with an electric quickness, or physical action, which operates with mechanical speed.

Consider in the recitation or singing of the psalms that we are not merely the recipients of their grace, but that we, in turn, send them (the psalms) through us and back to their source. In this complete circuit, we both pray and are prayed, re-creating prayer as we pray.

Dwelling in Your house
Is happiness,
But offering praise to You
Is better still, *selah!*

For those who
Are at home with You,
There is satisfaction;
And for those who
Have You as their God,
There is serenity.

Everyday I offer
You my praise
And remember
You in all that I do;
For You are
Truly magnificent,
And Your greatness is
Beyond all knowing.

Generation
After Generation
Tells its experience of You
To the next;
Splendid and Glorious
Is Your Name among us.

Gate to the Heart

My God,
My only Sustenance!
I hold You above,
And remember You before
All that I do.

My delight
Is to speak of You;
While others tell
Of Your awesome Power,
I praise Your
Overwhelming Kindness;
You are Gentle
And Compassionate,
Patient and Caring
With me, always.

Indeed, You are
Good to all of us;
All that You have made
You hold in Your Tenderness.

You fashioned us
To be Your devotees,
To bless You
And to speak
Of the honor
Of Your Realm,
To draw our energy
From Your Power;
We are the heralds
Of Your Uniqueness
And Your Majesty.

You embrace
The Universes;

Your authority
Flows through
And binds every
Generation.

You keep us
From faltering
And help us up
When we stumble;
So we all look
To You, Hopeful,
Trusting in
Your Providence,
Guiding us
In the right moment
To what we really need.

You open Your hand
And each of us receives
What we truly desire.

You are a *Tzaddik*
In all Your ways,
A *Hasid* in all
That You do!

You are close by
When we call on You,
Shaping our will
And our awareness,
Hearing our
Plaintive voices
With Your help.

You protect those
Who are Your lovers

And dissolve
The negativity
Of those who have
Gone astray.

I offer my mouth
To God's praise;
May all bodies of flesh
Bless Your holy Name
For as long as there is
Life on this world.

GUIDANCE:

Praying the Psalms

HERE ARE SOME suggestions for entering into a psalm or prayer. If you *davven* alone, wrap yourself in a *tallit*, or 'prayer-shawl,' and begin to read the psalm slowly with chant and expression. Make the sound beautiful and rich, the body posture an accompaniment to the words, the face in harmony with the words to be spoken. Then, close your eyes and visualize the scene surrounding the words, and placing yourself in King David's palace, recite them as he might have when he first composed them.

Do you find yourself in the prayer? Or, in the case of one of the psalms, are you really exhorting all creation to praise God? Are you the sky and the sun and the moon praising? Are you the flora and fauna? Are you the kings or queens of the earth, the old people and children?

With each *halleluyah* simulate that praising creature in some way. Are you just out of Egypt, redeemed by God, led dry-shod through the split sea? Treat the text as a model for adoration. Each time you mention the music of an instrument, become that instrument; hear it on the inside and offer the consciousness of the sound to God.

∞

THE PRAYER OF KNOWING — BE'RIYAH

NOW, WHEN WE come to the *Yotzeir Or*, we move to another realm. This realm, tradition tells us, is about the angels, about the lights of the day, and so on. We speak of *Serafim*, the creatures of fire, the *Hayyot* and other orders of angels and divine beings. They all stand in awe of the Divine, and say, *Kadosh, Kadosh, Kadosh!* "Holy, Holy, Holy!"

Then I go still higher into the place where we recite the *Sh'ma'*. At this point, prayer is more gentle, and the melodies become more head melodies than heart melodies. Here, we recalibrate ourselves with those things that we must never forget:

> Listen, Yisra'el,
> 'God-wrestler,'
> *Yah* Who is,
> Is our God;
> *Yah* Who is,
> Is One, Unique,
> All there is.

Through time and space,
Your glory shines,
O Majestic One!

Love *Yah,* your God,
In what your
Heart is invested,
In what you aspire to,
In what you have
Made your own.

May these words
And values
I connect with
Your life today,
Be implanted
In your heart.

May they become
The conscious-norm
For your children;
Express them
In the intimacy
Of your home,
As you go out walking,
Pursuing your errands;
May they guide you
In your rest, in relaxation,
And energize you
With wakefulness
And productivity.

Bind them as a sign
On your arm,
Let them be a beacon
Before your eyes,
Focusing your attention
And insight.
Inscribe them
On all your transitions,
On all your thresholds,
At home, and in
Your environment.

∞

How good it will be
When you really listen
And hear the directions
I give you today
For loving *Yah*
Who is Your God,
Acting godly,
With all your
Heart's feeling,
And all your
Soul's inspiration.

Then,
Your earthly needs
Will be met
At the right time,
And the rains
Will descend
In their season;

You will reap
What you plant
For your delight
And health;
Your animals will have
Ample sustenance;
All of you will eat
And be content.

Be aware, watch out!
Don't let your cravings
Delude you;
Don't become alienated;
Don't let your cravings
Become your gods;
Don't debase yourself
Before them,
Because the God-sense
Within you
Will become distorted;
Heaven will be
Shut to you,
Grace will not descend,
And Earth will not yield
Her produce;
Your rushing
Will destroy you!
And Earth will not be able
To recover Her
Good balance
In which God's gifts
Manifest.

May these words,
These values of Mine
Reside in your
Heart-feelings
And soul-aspirations,
Bind them as signs
On your arms,
Marking what you produce,
Let them be a beacon
Before your eyes,
Guiding what you Perceive.

Teach them to
Your children
So that they are
Instructed
In how to make
Their homes sacred,
In how to deal
With the traffic
Of life outside.

May these values
Of Mine reside
In your heart-feelings
And soul-aspirations;
When you are depressed,
And when you are elated.

Mark your entrances
And exits with them,
So you will be more
Aware.

Then, you and
Your children
And their children
Will live out on Earth
That Divine promise
Given to your ancestors,
To live heavenly days
Right here on this Earth.

∞

Yah Who Is
Said to Moses:
Speak, telling Israel to
Make *tzitzit*
On the corners
Of their garments,
So they will have
Generations
To follow them;
On each *tzizit*-tassel
Let them set
A sea-blue thread;
These *tzitzit* are
For your benefit!
Glance at them;
And in your seeing
Remember all the
Other directives of
Yah Who Is,
And act on them!

In this way
You will not be led astray,
Craving to see and want,
Prostituting yourself
For your cravings.

In this way
You will be mindful
And actualize
These directions
For becoming
Dedicated to your God;
To be aware *that*
I am *Yah* Who Is
Your God,
Who is the One
Who freed you
From oppression
In order to God you;
I am *Yah* Who Is
Your God,
That is the Truth.

∞

GUIDANCE:

Praying the Sh'ma'

To say the Sh'ma' more deeply and truly, try this exercise in your personal prayer, or with friends who will understand your intentions. Recite *El melekh ne'eman,* 'God, trustworthy king,' 26 times before saying the *Sh'ma'*. Then, when you come to the end of your 26 repetitions, pronounce the *Sh'ma'* with all your present intentions, becoming aware of them as you do it very slowly.

Sh'ma'—'hear,' understand, and in the hearing, make your *ayin*, the final letter of the word, big! *Yisra'el*—'God-wrestler,' you, the person, one of the 600,000 letters of God's Torah. *Y-H-V-H—Adonai*—all the levels of reality in which God Gods forever and always. *Eloheinu*, 'our God,' our nature and our being in God's being. This *Y-H-V-H* is, was, and will be *Ehad*, one, unique, altogether, infinitely loving 'One.'

Now, omit the word '*Yisra'el*,' and substitute your own name for it. Say it again with all the significance and meaning it has when you address it to your own situation, with your own concerns.

Now, say the *Sh'ma'* again, and this time, instead of *Yisra'el*, put the name of a person to whom your heart wishes to send this message, and say it addressing that person most lovingly, speaking from your own truth.

Now, visualize yourself on your own deathbed, wanting to leave the world with one last statement before you pour your whole life-experience into God's ocean of consciousness. Or, even more intensely, you might imagine yourself with a group of Jews in a gas chamber. You cannot escape the fact that this is the end, so you join them in one last shout . . . "*Sh'ma'*!"

Now imagine the expansion of the universe is done. God is reabsorbing it, taking it back into the Eternal Being, and this galaxy is plunging into a black hole. As you say the *Sh'ma'* now, imagine your voice and awareness merging with that of a universe dipping into the infinite *mikveh* of God.

Then, after you have gone with your heart and mind to all these places, say the *Sh'ma'* a fifth time bringing all the four situations together. When you have done this, you will have the sense of what the kabbalists used to call a *yihud*—a 'unification.'

∞

🗲

THE PRAYER OF BEING — ATZILUT

AFTER THIS COMES the highest point of the service when we get in touch with a level of deep intuition in the *Amidah*. In the traditional liturgy, there is a 'dipping down' of feeling between the prayers of the *Sh'ma'* and the prayers which lead into the *Amidah*, as though the prayers of *Ezrat Avoteinu*, the 'Help of our Parents,' and what follows, are an afterthought.

The *Amidah* is the prayer of *Atzilut*. *Atzilut* is not doing, feeling or knowing; it is '*Be-ing*.' And the prayer of *Be-ing* is stillness. As with prophet Elijah's experience of the wind, the quaking, and the fire—*Y-H-V-H* was not in them, but in the *kol d'mammah dakkah*, the "sound of subtle stillness" (often translated as, "a still small voice") (1 Kings 19:12).

When I try to be still, even for a few seconds, I quickly lose myself in worries or concerns. I then see that this is something I need to pray about, and thus I bring these worries and concerns to God in the words of the *Amidah*— "forgive," "redeem," "heal," "make prosper," etc. In this way, the words of the *Amidah* point to raising one's concerns with God. However, in between the rising of concerns in me, I may be able to find and maintain the stillness again.

And in that stillness, *Ehyeh asher Ehyeh,* "I Am that I Am" (Ex. 3:14) is there—*Is-ing.*

REFLECTION:

The Amidah's Silence

WHY DO WE DO the *Amidah* silently? Because the greatest thing we can do is to offer our stillness to God, to make ourselves so transparent to the Infinite that the ego doesn't offer any resistance. But since this is difficult, the *Amidah* consists of all of the things which come up in a person's mind: "I am so blessed to have had ancestors which created and passed on to me a tradition of seeking God." "I am aware of the cycle of life and death." "When I still myself, I feel Holiness." "I am trying to quiet myself, so that I can place all of my awareness in the right place, so that I can harmonize myself, so that I can be forgiven my sins." And so the *Amidah* unfolds. But better even than just the recital of the individual prayers is to return after each blessing to the stillness, and then resume the formal prayer only when you can't hold the stillness anymore. It's a very strong practice.

∞

The *Amidah* begins, *"Yah,* open my lips and my mouth will declare Your praise" (Ps. 51:15). Rather than seeing myself as a supplicant before God, I try to visualize myself as *seen* by God as I say these prayers. I become object, and God subject, rather than remaining a subject opposite and apart from God.

This merging with God is what the *Atzilut* level of consciousness entails. It is as if I were to say that I look from the Divine perspective at how Zalman is praying. When I say, *Sh'ma' koleinu,* "Hear our voice," I have to be the *Shome'a Te'fillah,* the one who hears prayer, as it were. My ears and my mouth serve God because I've said to God: "This 'instrument' is at your disposal. 'Open my lips and my mouth will declare Your praise.' What would you have me say?"

And God says: "I want you to be the high priest for yourself, for your *mishpahah* (family), for the world, and make those requests necessary for human life. And when you come to *Sim shalom tovah u'vrakhah,* 'Grant peace, goodness and blessing,' I want you to really bring *shalom* down."

The ideal is to strive to be the one who 'hears' as well as the one who 'prays' in the *Amidah.* But we need to be able to say here that, in order to live life well, we need *hokhmah, binah, da'at,* 'wisdom,' 'understanding,' 'knowledge,' and a list of other qualities and substances. I need *t'shuvah,* 'repentence' and harmony, I need *ge'ula sh'lemha,* 'complete redemption.' I need *refu'ah,* 'healing.' I need *parnassa,* 'livelihood.' I need all these things.

MEDITATION:
*Kabbalistic Affirmations
based on the Amidah*

I affirm the power
Of positive affirmations;
I affirm the *Shekhinah*—
Surrounding and
Blessing me;

I affirm the light-beings
Of God's service,
Who support
And guide me.

AVOT

I affirm the blessings
Of Abraham and Sarah
In my life.

TE'HIYAH

I affirm the
Sacrifice of Isaac,
And God's power
Over my life
And my death.

KE'DUSHAH

I affirm
God's holiness,
And my growth
Toward it.

SHOVER OYVIM

I place myself
Under the protection
Of the *se'firah* of *keter*,
Which will shield me
From all harm
And nullify it.

Atah Honen

I invoke the
Influx of *hokhmah*,
To align my intellect
With clarity and purpose,
To inspiration
And realization.

Hashiveinu

I invoke the
Care of *binah*
To lead me to the
Heart of Holiness.

Se'lihah

I invoke the
Abundance of *hesed*,
To bring me
To atonement.

Ge'ullah

I invoke the
Power of *ge'vurah*,
To see me through
All trouble
And lead me
To redemption.

הוּ

REFU'AH

I place myself in
The compassionate heart
Of God's *tiferet,*
And affirm the
Healing, balancing,
Integrative, and
Centering light
Within me.

BRAKHAH, MASHIAH, SHEKHINAH

I support myself on
The pillar of *netzah,*
Channeling to me
All manner of blessings
And prosperity,
Which I place
At the disposal
Of the redeeming *Mashiah,*
Unfolding to witness
The Shekhinah's
Residing in Zion.

הּ

KIBBUTZ GALUYOT, YERUSHALAYIM, MODIM

I support myself on
The pillar of *hod,*
Making order in my life,

Gathering all the forces
From dispersion
And settling them
In blessed Jerusalem,
Where I offer my thanks
To God's Glory.

Tzedakah U'mishpat, Tzaddikim, Shalom

I base myself
On the foundation
Of *yesod,*
To act righteously
And justly;
To assist in every
Righteous effort
In the world,
And to become
Peaceful in the work
Of peace.

הֹ

Shome'a Te'fillah

I affirm that *malkhut,*
The *Shekhinah,*
Is the one offering
These affirmations
In me...
And is attracting
The flow of blessings,
Which suffuses my life.
Amen . . . Amen.

∞

BRINGING DOWN THE DIVINE INFLUX — YERIDAT HA'SHEFA

IN COMING TO A CLOSE, at the end of the prayer service, we recite the *Aleinu*. As we say, *ve'anahnu kor'im u'mishtahavim u'modim*, "And we bend the knee and bow down and give thanks," we are back on the ground again. We are on our way out into the world with the concluding lines, *ba'yom hahu yehiyeh Ha'Shem ehad u'sh'mo ehad*, "and in that day, Yah will be one, and God's name will be one."

When we close with *Adon Olam* or another hymn, we have set the tone for whatever comes to us during the day. Now you have a sense of what the journey up and down that the *davvenen* was meant to be.

REFLECTION:
Attunement in Prayer

THERE WAS A TIME when people felt that the relationship they had to God was one of servant to Master. There are many passages in our liturgy that speak in this way. In such a relationship, the servant attends upon the Will of the Master, taking orders as they are commanded.

Another orientation in prayer that we have regarded as primary has been as children speaking with a parent. But this also does not satisfy the more intimate feeling in which we conceive of our relationship with the Divine as a search for the Beloved—a search that is also the Beloved's search for us.

Consider, too, our very act of praying. If we conceive

---

of God as Omniscient, it begins to appear somewhat absurd, this act of human prayer. If God knows all, why do we need to communicate with God in prayer? And if God doesn't know, again, what's the use of praying? We clearly aren't praying in order to inform or confirm.

Suppose, then, that our primary purpose is to join the angels and archangels in praise of God. Yet, even this does not seem right to us at this point in history.

Perhaps, in our extremity, it begins to dawn on us that we are in a relationship of identity with the Divine. *We are God.* But this identity creates a terrible confusion, because we see ourselves in two ways, both as ego and as Divine.

For this, I once I heard a powerful *mashal*, a 'parable,' from Eli Wiesel:

> Once, God and the human being had a dialogue.
>
> The human being said to God: "It's not fair that you are always God, and I am always the human being. If we are really partners, I should get a chance to be God, and You should be the human being."
>
> And God said: "I'm afraid. I'm afraid that you won't be able to handle it." Then the human being, who is such a fine seducer, seduced God in a weak moment and God said, "Okay."
>
> And both of them went crazy—God because God is now finite with God's infinitude, and the human being because the human being is now infinite within finity! They have been trying to meet again, to switch back, ever since.

Perhaps our primary service in prayer is now to the

Earth, to the environment, to ecological awareness. We have taken so much from Nature that we must now be aware of Her needs. We must turn in new directions with our prayers, engaging unexplored parts of our soul in worship.

∞

MUSIC AND PRAYER

JUST AS THERE IS A PATH to the heart that goes via the nose, for which we use incense and perfume, so there is a path that goes from the ear to the heart, for which we have music. In Judaism, there have been the traditional sound-paths of cantillation, giving us the denotative majors of Torah reading and talmudic study of *halakhah*, or Jewish law, and the connotative minors of the tropes of the Prophets and the chant of studying the non-legal Aggadic portions of the Talmud.

Nussah is the term used for the different melodic modes of *davvenen* used for weekday, *Shabbat* and *Yom Tov* chants, as well as several High Holiday modes, each designed to take the worshipper into the universe of discourse of the particular time and its prayer.

There are also *niggunim* (sing. *niggun*), or 'melodies,' which one can learn and use according to the essence which they mediate in relation to prayer. The traditional *Shalom Aleikhem* and *Eliyahu ha'Navi* ushering in the *Shabbat* and the week are such bridges of consciousness. There are, of course, more sophisticated ones, and these can be learned from classical and current Hasidic *niggunim* collections. There are also one's own 'doors' that have been fashioned by classical and modern music. Each person who can use the path of sound has his or her own favorites.

A collage of mood-inducing pieces can really help in difficult transitions. So, if, during the last preparations for *Shabbat*, one wishes to play such music that enhance the change from the weekdays to the *Shabbat*, this is desirable. It forms a *mikveh* of sound in which to immerse oneself. Such a bridge can also be of help everyday before prayer; as some Hasidim say, "The time of prayer, even during the weekday, is *Shabbat*." Likewise, a Hasidic dance can help in a vigorous transition from *davvenen* to work.

Whether you *davven* in English or Hebrew, *niggun* and *nussah* are vital links, adding other tracks to that of verbal consciousness. The more tracks which are added simultaneously, the more *kavvanah,* or 'intention,' enters the prayer, and the more the prayer reconstitutes the experience it once was before being written down.

The volume of sound in prayer and chanting ought to correspond to the energy-flow that feels right for the occasion. This applies to the tempo too. There are prayers that need an *allegro,* and others that need *lento* or *largo*. Practice with various tempi will be of help in allowing the right energy to be invested in the *davvenen*.

How God can be Found
Where God is Sought

This brings us to corporate worship at a *shul,* a synagogue or prayer-meeting. At this point, you are aware of some of the valuable and uplifting material available in the traditional prayer service; but you may be impatient with some of the human factors in group prayer or synagogue worship—the officiating rabbi or cantor, or the other worshippers—might make your synagogue experience or prayer-meeting something less than inspiring. So, let's talk about how we can make the service a better resource for you.

Before leaving home, you should decide that you are not going to your place of worship in order to 'get something,' but rather to serve God. The 'getting' is not at all important when you come to serve. You serve by active participation in reading, chanting and listening. You intend that these activities are pleasing to God. As you enter the *shul*, avoid any conversation. Your time before the service is best used in active and passive meditation, petition, intercession and preparation.

In the Jewish tradition, we have always sought to pray with a *minyan*, a quorum of ten people. It is important because we want the *Shekhinah*, or Divine Presence, to be at our prayer-meeting—*Akol dibei assara Shekhinta sharya*, "Where there are ten, there the *Shekhinah* is present."* Ten people are considered the social critical mass for the manifestation of the Divine Presence. According to the Kabbalah, we need ten people so that all the *se'firot*, divine qualities, will be represented and activated. So, as soon as the *minyan* is assembled, you are assured that God is present. Don't worry about the problem of God's particular Presence in the face of God's Omnipresence. Someday you will know the difference. Just be assured that there is a difference, and that with the *minyan*, God is here in a manner approximating God's Presence in the Holy of Holies in the Temple.

With this Presence, you can do quite a bit. You address God in God's *Shekhinah* and grow in worship. But you also remember that God's *Shekhinah* is contingent on the other worshippers. They are the ones who bring God's Presence to you, and you must love them in it. You, therefore, affirm your love for all the worshippers at the beginning of the service. If you find this difficult, you can at least affirm your wish to love them.

---

* Sanhedrin 39a.

Now, as the service begins, you enter into the spirit of the worship as-it-ought-to-be. You might read the prayers as actors reads their lines, putting feeling and conviction into your chanting. In worship, it need not be you who speaks— you can become David's mouthpiece. The liturgy speaks for you, with you acting as an instrument. Make sure that you know the often used congregational responses; then you can partake in them naturally.

The plural which you use in the liturgy may represent the congregation, but also the many levels of your own awareness. Thus, the liturgy becomes effective as a unitive power. The *Aron Kodesh*—the Holy Ark in which the Torah scroll is housed—should be your focus. Visualize the Divine Presence there. When it is opened, you might send prayers in that direction.

If possible, study the liturgy with a teacher or friend and learn how to expand its meaning to accommodate a higher level of *kavvanah*. By becoming aware of the many levels of insightful *kavvanah*, you enlarge your intentional repertoire. A person with a diversified repertoire of *kavvanot* can serve in many moods and spiritual 'keys.'

The liturgical year of the *siddur* and *mahzor* makes demands on one's ability to sing in the 'key' which the time and season demand. This holds true not only concerning chant, but also concerning the inner mood and approach to these seasons. Be sure to pray privately before corporate worship that God may grant you the resources you need for serving God in the group prayer.

During the Torah reading, pay attention, intending to hear in it the solution to your current problems. Follow the Torah reading closely and hope for at least one sentence or part per week to speak to you, personally. Treasure this sentence, and work with it for the whole week.

When hearing the sermon, pray to God that there may be something important in it for you. Your sympathetic attention and expectation to hear a living word will have its own effect on the speaker. Any word which you feel is useful to you, remember and treasure, for God sent it to you through the speaker. You might, when hearing some statements which you can affirm, shout aloud inside yourself, "*Amen!*"

After the service is over, you might wish to remain seated for another few moments, 'tarrying awhile.' You need not become conspicuous. It just takes a few minutes for the congregation to file out.

You might also want to visit the *shul* from time to time in order to meditate. Despite the fact that it may be empty, or perhaps because of it, you may gain something worthwhile.

REFLECTION:
The Tracks of Consciousness in Worship

IN MOST PLACES OF WORSHIP these days there exists a conspiracy. Public worship and prayer are ostensibly carried out there but on deeper inspection, one finds that they are actually sabotaged. The social expectations of the regular synagogues diametrically oppose the words of the prayer-book: "Sing unto God a new song," "Let us kneel and bow down before God, our Maker," "Shout for joy and clap your hands" are merely *said* and not *done*.

Real emotion is discouraged, even at *Yizkor*, the traditional mourning service. There are no tears on Yom Kippur, nor on Tish'a b'Av, and no celebrating on Simhat Torah, nor on Purim.

Clearly, we may want to change all this for ourselves so that we can gain the benefits of attending a public service while making the synagogue visit a spiritually momentous experience. If we have the inner imaginative space that meditation has carved-out inside of our awareness, this is not only possible, but even deeply fulfilling to the soul.

Please follow me a bit now with concerned awareness and an awakened heart. You are now reading text. This is track *Alef* of consciousness. You have 'tuned' in your concern to get into the spirit of worship. This is track *Beit*. You have (as if) said to your heart, "Keep hoping, heart, that maybe there is something nourishing for you in these lines." That is track *Gimmel*. Now get in touch with your questions—track *Dallet*. Read the next lines with all these tracks out loud—with melody track *Heh* ...

Ahat sha'alti m'eth Adonai,
A unique thing I ask of the Lord,
Ot'hah avakkesh,
This thing is my quest,
Shiviti b'veth Adonai,
To be at home in the Lord's house,
Kol y'mei hayyai,
All the days of my life.

You have now covered six tracks of awareness. Add to them the tracks of meaning and intention, the tracks of Hebrew and English, as well as the tracks of body movement, tensing and flexing—infusing the words with an energy that feels true and right to the meaning, and which participates in the many tracks of significance coming from your own life-situation.

On this we impose the awesome track of being in the Presence of the Infinite, while the phantom body dances the dance that belongs to the words. Further and deeper over the intervening millennia, you are also David hunted in the world, intended for a royal palace and yearning only to make yourself present in God's sanctuary. So you are David's mouthpiece, as well as that of all your ancestors, who, in so many different settings in the world, have entered these words with fervor and longing—people for whom the Psalms were the language of dialogue with God. So, from time-to-time, before and during worship, allow yourself to scan as many of these tracks of consciousness as you can.

∞

Ritual Objects in Judaism

Introduction

WE DON'T WANT RITUAL OBJECTS to be the sole connection we have to God, becoming personal idols to us; but we are nevertheless human beings with bodies that respond to external stimuli.

In the body, the final letter of the divine name, the final *Heh* of *Y-H-V-H*, represents action in the material universe, and thus also behaviorism is the one's psychology. Therefore, the more we can create stimuli that promote and entrain repetition and focus in us, locating us in time and space, the better.

TALLIT & TZITZIT

TRADITION HAS GIVEN US the *tallit*, the prayer-shawl, a blanket for our aura, providing us with a safe space in which we can be cozy with God. These feelings of comfort are similar to those of the child who wants to bring everyone together under one blanket, so that the whole family can share the warmth.

But the *tallit* is also the four-cornered garment whose fringes, or *tzitzit*, are meant to remind us of the 613 *mitzvot*. The *tzitzit* are, as Reb Arthur Waskow has so beautifully put it, "the bleed-off of the field into the environment." Recognizing this, my friend, the artist, Menahem Alexenberg, has also built a school in Yeruham, from the four corners of which hang heavy rope *tzitzit* that run into the sand! This is a way of saying, "Yes, I am safe here; I am grounded in this environment."

EXPLANATION:

The B'nai Or Tallit

"HOW DID GOD CREATE LIGHT? God wrapped in a *tallit* and it began to shine."*

It was this *midrash* that inspired me to design the now well-known rainbow striped B'nai Or Tallit, each color of which represents one of the *se'firot*, or divine emanations, through which God's energy becomes manifest in the world.

---

* *Midrash Rabbah,* Be'reshit 3:4.

The *atarah*—the embroidered strip at the neck of the *tallit*—represents *keter*, the 'crown,' the source of God-energy, which flows into *hokhmah* and *binah*, represented by the white of the *tallit* itself. These three 'upper' *se'firot* represent divine energy beyond human comprehension.

From there, the energy flows into the 'lower seven' *se'firot*. Each of these corresponds to some aspect of the Divine, and to one of the days of creation.

The purple stripes represent *hesed*, 'loving-kindness,' and the first day of creation, *be'reshit*. The deep purple stripe suggests ultra-violet light emerging from total darkness. The lighter purple stripe, with some white mixed in it, symbolizes the light becoming visible. This stripe is very wide because the nature of *hesed* is broad and sweeping. Thus, it needs strong black lines to contain it.

The next stripe is *tekhelet*-blue, representing *gevurah*, 'rigor,' and the second day of creation when the sky, the blue fluids above, were separated from the blue sea-waters below.

Following the creation story, the third stripe is green like chlorophyll, representing *tiferet*, 'beauty,' and the creation of vegetation. God said, "It is good" (Gen. 1:10, 12) twice on the third day, so there are two green stripes with the white light of *keter* coming through the middle. *Tiferet* needs a vessel, so there are black lines containing it.

The yellow stripe represents *netzah*, 'victory,' and the fourth day, when the moon, stars and sun—a yellow star—were created.

Next is the orange stripe, representing *hod,* 'glory,' and the fifth day when the fish, reptiles, birds and insects were created. Because these are all egg-laying animals, the stripe is the color of egg-yolk.

There is a close relationship between *netzah* and *hod*, with different kabbalistic systems interpreting them in different ways. There is no glory *(hod)* without victory *(netzah)*.

The sixth stripe is red and represents *yesod*, 'foundation,' and the sixth day of creation when the warm-blooded animals were created. As chlorophyll is the blood of plants, hemoglobin is the blood of animals, so the stripe is blood red. *Yesod* also represents sexuality and needs strong black lines to contain it.

The final stripe represents *malkhut*, 'sovereignty,' and the creation of human beings from humus, earth. This stripe is brown because all living things come from earth and return to earth when they die.

As I mentioned, the black lines and white stripes have meaning. The black lines border those *se'firot* which need strong boundaries to contain their energy. But, some of the *se'firot*, like *gevurah* and *malkhut* do not need the lines, because they are themselves containers.

∞

TE'FILLIN

THE TWO SMALL LEATHER BOXES containing verses from Torah (Ex. 13:1-10, 11-16; Deut. 6:4-9, 11:13-21) written on parchment by hand are called *te'fillin*. *Te'fillin* are made of rawhide and sewn with sheep gut. Each box is attached to long leather straps. One is wound around the arm and hand, and the other is placed on the head. Every letter is hand-written. Of course, printing would produce the information, but it would not produce the act of making the *te'fillin*. The fact that everything has to be hand-made in the *te'fillin* tells us that even in the most technologically advanced societies we are not to use nylon thread to fasten with, but rather handspun gut. Hand-written also means that it is written in a particular order. In the *te'fillin*, you may not write a later letter first; it has to be written *ke'sidran*, in order.

When I ask a *sofer*, 'scribe,' to write a pair of *te'fillin* for a grandchild of mine, or a *mezuzah* for a friend, I ask them to have particular *kavvanot*, or 'intentions,' in mind that when they come to particular words. That is to say, to bring consciousness through the materials and process. If I say that silicon chips create the possibility for the flow of certain kinds of memories and ideas, then you can also understand how parchment with this writing, with the Divine Names upon it, has been that technology for us.

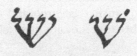

GUIDANCE:
Phantom Te'fillin

WHEN I TEACH PEOPLE how to put on *te'fillin*, I often ask them to put on "phantom *te'fillin*" for a week first. That is, to refrain from putting them on in actuality at first, but to pretend to put them on, keeping their minds on them, and training themselves to let them be *le'ot al-yadekha ul'totafot bein einekha*, "a sign on your arm and a reminder-ribbon on your forehead."

I show them, for instance, where to put the *shel yad*, the arm *te'fillin*, which goes near the heart on the muscle close to the chest on the left arm (or right arm, if you are left handed). Then I ask them to take, in their imagination, a beam of neon light that begins with the purples and goes via the blues, greens, yellows, oranges down to the reds of the spectrum, as they make the seven windings around the forearm, from the elbow to the wrist.

Putting on the *shel rosh*, the head *te'fillin* in the same way, I suggest visualizing the Hebrew letter *Shin* on the left of the imaginary box, and a *Shin* on the right. The *Shin* on the left has four prongs, the *Shin* on the right has three—three standing for synthesis, four standing for analysis—cerebellum and occiput (fore and aft of head) and where the knot is, the corpus callosum connecting the two. Think of all the neurons together in the service of God, your affect and your action being in the service of God. Sit with that for a little while. Then, take them off, as it were, and wrap the non-physical *te'fillin*, putting them away in a non-physical bag for a while.

In the middle of the day you can reach for these non-physical *te'fillin* and go through the meditation. For, originally, the *tallit* and *te'fillin* were worn all day, as what they help us remember are most needed when we are outside of the house of worship and our prayer-spaces.

∞

Mezuzah

As we move from one space into another, we want to do so consciously. And that is what a *mezuzah* is for. It provides an opportunity for a conscious transition. Here is the fulfillment of the Biblical injunction to "write them on the doorposts of your house" (Deut. 6:9; 11:20), just as the *te'fillin* fulfill the commandment "that they be as a sign upon your arm and between your eyes" (Deut. 6:8; 11:18).

THE BEDTIME SH'MA'

INTRODUCTION

ONE WHO WISHES to create an inner life of the spirit and prayer must make the *Sh'ma'* before bedtime its devotional basis. This prayer is designed to be said in solitude, while all other prayers (*Ma'ariv*, *Shaharit*, and *Minha*) are basically communal prayers, best said in a quorum of ten or more—a *kahal*, a *minyan*. The bedtime *Sh'ma'* differs from these other prayers in that it is a very 'private' act of worship between the individual soul and God. Elsewhere, one can find ample discussion of the historic development of this prayer.* Our concern here is to describe its function and purpose.

Basically, this prayer is an examination of conscience at a time when such an examination may bring positive results, i.e., before retiring for the night. However, it is not enough simply to prepare one's spiritual ledger sheet. One must also be willing and able to do something with the information which is thus gained. One must be able to mend one's relationship to God and people, and be able to exert such influence as is necessary to 'right' one's life.

---

* See Adin Steinsaltz, *A Guide to Jewish Prayer*, New York: Schocken Books, 2000:101-03.

One needn't spend more than five to ten minutes on this process. It is just necessary to check through our actions to see if they were as we planned them to be. Once a week—Thursday night might be best—you should set aside more time than usual for a more thorough examination of conscience. Do this when you are still fresh. If you leave it until you are too worn out, you cannot expect to succeed.

MEDITATION:
Examination of Conscience

BEFORE RETIRING FOR THE NIGHT, begin the practice of *heshbon ha'nefesh*—'soul-reckoning.' To start, you must fully and completely forgive anyone who has wronged or hurt you at any time—whether intentionally or unintentionally—and pray for their welfare. Check on your relationships, recalling whatever frustration or hurt was experienced during the day at the hands of others. Imagine them as written on slips of paper and rip these up, one-by-one, forgiving fully those who have hurt you, as you say these words:

Master of the Universe,
I wish to forgive
Whoever has hurt
Or wronged me,
Whether deliberately
Or by accident,
Whether by
Word or deed,
In this incarnation
Or in previous ones;
I pray that no one be
Harmed on my account.

May it be Your Will,
Yah, my God,
God of my forbears,
That I err no more,
That I do not revert
To my old ways,
That I do not
Anger You anymore
By my actions;
May I no longer do
What is evil in Your sight.

Please, wipe clean
The negative impressions
That I have left
On others this day
With the Strength
Of Your Compassion,
But not through
Sickness or suffering.

May the words
Of my mouth,
And the prayers
Of my heart
Be acceptable
To You,
My Rock
And my Redeemer.

Then you make a short tally of your actions throughout the day, either beginning with the first thought upon waking (this thought is of tremendous power, exerting a powerful influence on the entire day), or 'walking backward' in your mind through the day to its start.

As you do this, try to feel the Divine Presence in your being, and begin to judge yourself in God's sight—not harshly, not carelessly, but justly. And do this in detail. Don't condemn or convict yourself; but visualize yourself before God and listen to God's *just* judgment.

When you have finished with this process, offer all your 'sins' and guilt up to God. Ask God to take these from you, and to wash you clean.

Now, at this point, you might move into the higher feeling of remorse, and be more pained for what you've done to the Beloved than for impeding your own progress. You might read from one of the Psalms a few times (perhaps Psalm 20, 25, 51, 73, or 130). Then renew your covenant with God and prepare for bed.

∞

In this process, it is helpful to have an image which you can use to arouse the Infinite Mercy. This arousing of God's Mercy is called *hit'or'rut rah'mim rabbim*. Consider these images: the sullied and fallen prince or princess returning to face the loving Royal Parent; or the amnesiac, exiled prince or princess, who suddenly remembers his or her true identity; or the man or woman, who, for love, has been saving every penny to ransom their beloved, and who has just been robbed of that hard-earned money; or the prisoner, made to help his or her oppressors; the child who has lost his or her parents in the crowd because he or she was looking at puppies in the pet store window; the spark which wants to return to the flame . . . but cannot.

The purpose of such imagery is to help us feel the need of God's Mercy, to feel our helplessness in God's Presence, and, in the utter inability to do anything to help ourselves, to implore God in language that is our own. This utter 'helplessness' before God is not a theological dogma; but a functional attitude appropriate for this stage of spiritual development.

The real power in this practice, and many others, only begins to show after you can control the sequence of thoughts and feelings. Though it may come easily at first, it demands great persistence to rebuild intangibles that years of driven-ness have undone. Nevertheless, you will succeed with persistence.

You will find that a number of verses in prayer should be repeated at least three times. This is not done merely to amass words; but rather, to soak one's soul in a particular emphasis. Three times is not a limit, but an opportunity. In the *Sh'ma'* at bedtime, we utilize such verses to infuse the virtues of hope, trust and blessed reliance on God into our body and mind, to get them to relax ever more fully.

Learn to say the *Sh'ma'* in your native tongue, feeling it not literally; but rather, modified by Hasidic insights and intentions. Remember, when saying the *Sh'ma'*, to keep in mind all the intentions you have learned which deal with God's blessed Oneness:

MEDITATION:
Ha'Mapil and the Archangels

AFFIRM THE ONENESS OF GOD and our love for the One in the recitation of the *Sh'ma'*. Then, having recited the *Sh'ma'* while still fully dressed, undress and get ready for bed. Relax, making a conscious effort to lift your soul up and give it to God, saying the words of *Ha'Mapil,* and making

---

these the last words you speak before going to sleep:

Into Your Hands,
I entrust my soul
For the night;
You have redeemed me,
You do redeem me,
And will redeem me,
God of truth.

I offer You thanks,
Cosmic Majesty,
And worship You
Who casts the bands of sleep
Upon my eyes,
And sleepiness on my eyelids,
And yet, gives a soft,
Subtle light to the pupil
Of mine eye.

Now, as your eyelids start to become heavy, visualize your tensions departing, walking-out of your body, one-by-one, starting from your toes and eventually from between your eyes. Then, visualize your mattress as God's supporting Arms, feeling at the same time, caressed by God's Hand, as you say the final part of the prayer:

Please God,
God of my parents,
Will to make me
Lie down in peace,
And raise me up
To a good life of peace.

Please, do not allow
My dreams and fantasies,
Over which I have no control,
To confuse or upset me,
Or permit my thoughts
To defile me;
May my bed
Be harmonious with
Your Presence.

Give light to my eyes,
That I sleep not into death;
Blessed are You, *Yah,*
Who gives the light
Of Your Glory
To the world.

On other nights, after the examination of conscience, you might screen yourself in from sounds and cares by visualizing an angel—a spiritual force-field—of Grace at your right, a force-field impenetrable by care or worry; at your left, imagine yourself screened off by an angel of power and strength; before you, an angel of soft light and luminescence; behind you, an angel of healing; and over your head, picture the very Presence of God. As you visualize these, say:

In the name of *Yah,*
The God of Israel:
At my right hand, Mikha'el,
At my left hand, Gavri'el,
Before me, Uri'el,
Behind me, Rafa'el,
And above my head,
The *Shekhinah!*

> Imagine Mikha'el's gift of love, so that you can love more the next day; Gavri'el's gift of strength to fill you up for the next day; Uri'el's light of the mind; and Rafa'el's healing for all your ills.
>
> ∞

THE SOUL'S FLAW

IN ALL THIS TALK of 'soul-reckoning,' a word must be said about our 'blind-spot,' the way in which we conceal our true Self from ourselves, and conceal this act of concealment. This blind-spot is highly charged, and even as we catch a glimpse of it, it recedes, provoking all sorts of avoidant behaviors. However, if it is confronted and contained, it ultimately yields its secret and strength.

Sometimes, I like to talk about this as the soul's flaw. For every soul—*though truly a part of God's holy perfection*—is possessed of a 'flaw.' This flaw is not unlike the flaw in an opal, which creates its special 'fire,' its charm and attraction. The only difference between the 'fire' and the 'flaw' in the opal is in the refraction of light. Likewise, the soul's flaw can be a vice, or in different light, a virtue. The soul's main task is to work *on* and *with* that flaw.

The particular soul-trait which attracts people to it, and sparks something in them, is the same trait that is thought of as a flaw. Only, when it appears as a flaw, the special light in it has gone and, because of a shift in time and circumstances, the flaw remains unadorned. This flaw and its unique fire are two sides of the same configuration of the soul. Very few people have the ability to stay aware of their blind-spots. Even if they experience moments of awareness, they vanish quickly. One of the most crucial issues in the examination of one's conscience is the search for the awareness of one's basic flaw and fire.

There is no way to get away from the problems caused by the flaw. It takes great vigilance to learn to move the flaw into the right light where the fire in it begins to show. Often, it takes courageous work with a spiritual guide or friend to begin to reveal it and discern its outlines; but, in the end, only the person in whom it dwells can ultimately deal with it.

The flaw insinuates itself into every facet of our lives; and unfortunately, it is our failures—which are often so close to our successes—that tell us most about it. Moreover, the flaw is multi-leveled, so that even when one manages to control it in behavior, it shows itself again on the plane of feeling. And even if controlled there, it will continue to manifest on the plane of thought. Thus, it is a life-long relationship of struggle and revelation.

Making Love

MAKING LOVE IN A SACRED and committed relationship is the paradigm of the God-Israel relationship. Loving, intentional and conscious relating is a *mitzvah*, a double *mitzvah* when hoping to beget children. Kabbalists suggest that in making love we visualize the *Yud* and *Heh* of the Holy Name in constant embrace, while the letters *Vav* and *Heh* are oneself and one's partner—the *Vav* generally being regarded as the male partner, and the *Heh*, the female.

Reb Tzvi Elimelekh of Dynov asks the question, "Why don't we make a blessing over the enjoyment of making love? Since you cannot experience it without enjoying it, and to enjoy anything of this world without thanking God is not good, you should say in the common tongue,

'Thank you God for giving me a *mitzvah* which you cannot complete without feeling pleasure.' "*

Allow that pleasure to connect you with God in your heart, taking your time with the anthem of embraces and kisses. The holy Ba'al Shem Tov taught us that, "It was revealed to me from Above that the reason for the delay of the coming of the Messiah is that people don't enter enough into the mystery of kisses before the great loving." ***
Connect the consciousness of kissing to the kisses given to *tzitzit, mezuzah, Torah, te'fillin* and holy books.

When intending to bring a holy soul down into this world, pray that the Holy One and the *Shekhinah*, the Divine Presence, join you in the love-making. Visualize yourself in that heavenly sanctuary where Eliyahu, the prophet, connects parents and children, and commit yourselves to serving as hosts and educators to this new soul, to helping it in growing toward God.

After the descent from the holy Union, give thanks in a fitting way and share with your partner some holy insight gained. When alone, offer your longing and yearning to God as a form of compassion with the *Shekhinah* and Her longing for the Union with the One.

In the writings of the Rebbe of Baghdad, Rabbi Yosef Hayyim, author of *Ben Ish Hai,* we find this invocation before the sacred union:

> O that the beautiful Presence,
> In endless compassion,
> Would shed Her radiant
> Light upon us!

---

* Tzvi Elimelekh of Dynov, *Derekh Pikudekha,* in the section that deals with the first *mitzvah* to "be fruitful and multiply."
** Ya'akov Yosef of Polonoye, *Toldot Ya'akov Yosef*, Va'yera A.

GATE TO THE HEART

O that Your Will, God,
Most Exalted, in sound
And inflection encoded,
Would manifest in us!

O that the union,
Most total and sacred,
In infinite greatness would
Attain to the crowning!

We sprang from the Light-drop
Of the womb of the *Tzaddik*,
To grow to completion.

In this prayer,
We entreat You,
With the hope of our people,
That the blissful fulfillment
Send us its blessing.

O that the union,
Most holy, most sacred,
Be aroused to its peak,
As all power is sweetened!

May the root of the *Tzaddik*,
The way of the Sacred,
Find its completion
Right here and right now!

Through Time and Space
Your Glory shines,
Majestic One.

GUIDANCE:
The Mikveh

THE *MIKVEH* is the deepest preparation for holy acts. On the physical plane, we need to find a body of water that constitutes a *mikveh.** One usually takes newly laundered clothes along so that one may dress in them after the *mikveh*. Next, there is the washing in a shower before dipping. Then one dips once to remove the impurities acquired by body flows, touch, and entrance into impure spaces.

The next four dips are in the four directions: to the East, intending the letter *Yud* of the Divine Name; to the left, North, intending the upper *Heh*; to the West, intending the letter *Vav*; and to the South, intending the other *Heh*.

Each of the dips brings with itself *kavvanot* or 'intentions' on the spiritual level. Each one of the letters also refers to a universe, and the purification that is brought about by entering the *mikveh* on that level.

Special petitions are said in order between dips. When a *mikveh* is not available (with the exception of a woman's monthly purification), even a shower with these intentions is better than no *mikveh* at all.

∞

---

* For men, even a swimming pool can do for most occasions.

AN INTRODUCTION
TO SHABBAT

TEXTURE IN TIME

HOW DEEPLY PRECIOUS IS *SHABBAT*. If I were to be able to approach God now and give thanks, most of the holy gems on my life's garland of *Sheheheyanu* moments—peak experiences in which we thank God 'for having given us life'—for which I would give thanks, happened on *Shabbat*. It is the experience of *Shabbat* that has brought home to me the possibility of 'domesticating' peak experiences, to have a weekly date with the top values in my hierarchy. It is as if I work all week, *doing*, to earn the time I want to invest in *being*.

As I try to write about *Shabbat*, I feel the impossibility of it. Writing is a weekday occupation for me. The verb 'writing,' and the subject of the writing *Shabbat*, are in a negating mutuality. How did God engrave the fourth commandment regarding *Shabbat* on the tablets? Is there not some meeting-ground in which the week and the *Shabbat* do not relate by negation?

Yes! On Friday afternoon, all the busy-work is for the sake of *Shabbat*. The intention to rest is seemingly negated by all the feverish preparing; and yet, there is no contradiction. The *doing* is a phase of *being* and the *being* of *doing*.

Before *Kiddush*, we say *Yom Ha'shishi Vayekhulu Ha'shamayim*, "the sixth day, and the heavens were completed." Look at the initials of the words . . . They make the Divine Name, *Y-H-V-H*. The words, *Yom ha'shishi* belong to the end of chapter 1 in *Be'reshit* (Genesis) which deals with the six days in the *Yud* and *Heh* of God's Holy Name; but it is only on the *Shabbat* that the letters *Heh* and *Vav* become joined and the *Shabbat* completes the Name.

Whatever is grudging in me toward any creature, on *Erev Shabbat* suddenly turns to a wish to nurture it. There are, with the *Shabbat* eve, smells in the house, a sense of God's cornucopia of abundance, that are bigger than all the real and imagined needs I have, than all the past deprivations. This manages to relax in me—despite the urgency of the impending *Shabbat* and its accompanying busy-ness—all those muscles that chronically worry about tomorrow and yesterday.

The members of the household bump into each other in the bustle of the preparations, shining with the inner loveliness that we have when seen as we are, without expectations of the uses to which we are put in our battle with the Other Side. There comes also the sense of 'comrade-in-arms' as we smile at each other and give a happy touch in passing. Underneath is the awakening of *Eros* that imparts to the atmosphere a whiff of that Essence which fills late Spring nights with rich overflowing.

It begins to manifest in little touches of caring: 'Put the candles in this place so that they will shine their best,' or 'Check on that special dish.' Even in June, Friday afternoons do not allow enough time to prepare all that suggests itself to us for making *Shabbat* even more special and precious.

Shabbat is the day when we open the garden on the inside and meet God and our companions. The garden of the imagination, of tenderness and dreams, the garden in which grow fond memories and deep consolations. There are pools of being, fully understood and accepted, the flowers of appreciation, the secrets shared with songs and sunsets. There fly the birds of bliss and the butterflies that rise from the cocoons of the caterpillars of humiliation, illumined by the Light of the Gentle yet Infinite Presence.

Shabbat has always challenged the poet. The best thing that the kabbalist, Shlomo Halevi Alkabetz could say was, "Come, my beloved, and meet the Bride"—that's how we get to receive the inner realm of *Shabbat*.**

REFLECTION:

A Bit of the Coming World

WE SAY THAT *SHABBAT* is *me'ein Olam ha'Ba,* 'a bit of the coming world.' There is a teaching that says we take from the messianic future and invest in the present. Reb Pinhas of Koretz saw the Ba'al Shem Tov as the messianic light condensed and sent to keep us from fainting. Likewise, every *Shabbat* is a bit of the future condensed and brought into the present.

Shabbat is not for living in the past, 'driving by the rear view mirror.' It calls for seeing differently. One dreams of the future in terms of the trends of today, though some of these have not yet come to discernment.

In the soul exists the ability to visualize perfections that have not yet been manifested in this world—the spark of the Divine in us is not bound by the restrictions of time and space. On higher levels, in dimensions many times the power of ours, there are many more points of contiguity. This is what allows one to visit a time not yet come—the *Olam ha'Ba*—and to see visions there.

---

* *Lekhah Dodi,* a liturgical poem recited at dusk, or sundown for the arrival of *Shabbat.*

> Bringing them back to this set of dimensions, we can begin to initiate here the processes that will lead to the greater fulfillment. This indeed is the *Shabbat* and weekday cycle. On *Shabbat*, we envision as-yet-unrealized futures, and after *Havdalah*, at the close of *Shabbat*, we begin to move toward the realization-phases that are linked with the weekdays, anchored in the here and now.
>
> ∞

HOSPITALITY TO GOD

THE *SHABBAT* HAS TWO ASPECTS: the outer aspect of refraining from 'servile' work, as defined by the Mishnah (*Shabbat* 7:2), and subsequently by the codes of Jewish law; and the inner aspect of great effort in the direction of God, in Torah and prayer. In other words, work of another kind is indicated for the *Shabbat*. Instead of working with things on the outside, one must work with one's Self on the inside. After having been in a state of soul-reckoning, and its attendant bitterness, the *Shabbat* becomes a day of enjoying God.

To give yourself a framework for thinking about *Shabbat*, consider how the world is continually being created by God, how God's Will is continually *making* the world in which we exist. Nevertheless, there are many levels to that Will, many dimensions that parallel the human process. We 'will' something in our innermost being. This inner will works toward fulfillment; but often it has to be assisted by the outer, instrumental will, which sets up the mechanics of the fulfillment of the inner.

Let us say that we will to be in the state of sanctity and rest. In order to gain this inner will, we must work and hunger to acquire the means of eating and relaxing. So the outer will, which works toward fulfilling the inner will, is in exact opposition to the stated purpose so that it may achieve it.

Now picture God's Majesty, willing on the inner level to dwell with us in a *Shabbat*-like manner. In order to gain this, God creates a world with innumerable details to sustain us, and sustains innumerable people in order to have among them those who will invite God to dwell with them. During the week, the outer will is in ascendance, while the inner will is active only in a hidden way. Then, when *Shabbat* comes, the inner will comes to ascendance and the outer will remains in the background. This inner will, the real purpose of Creation, is to dwell with God. So here we have a framework for *kavvanah*. Every action on *Shabbat* must not be merely instrumental in preparing for God's dwelling, but must be an act of hospitality to God.

Now, we have to study the laws of *Shabbat* in order to know the framework of *Shabbat*. In this way, we learn to navigate its 26 hours.*

Guidance:
Shabbat Silence and Talk

SHABBAT IS PARTICULARLY DIFFICULT to experience and work-out in the absence of a friendly, intimate group, engaged in the same work. Nevertheless, we will concern

---

* For the sake of *kavvanah*, remember that the 26 hours of *Shabbat* correspond to the numerical value of the Divine Name, *Y-H-V-H*.

ourselves here with the individual. We must first remember to curb ordinary conversations on *Shabbat* and move inward. In refraining from doing and speaking in the ordinary way, we are able to do and speak inwardly. Only that which pertains to Torah and prayer in some way is proper conversation. Though the observance of mindful speech may seem stifling the first few times you attempt it, if you proceed out of an inner quietude, you will find other things speaking to—*in, with,* and *through*—you. Your prayer too, will become more alive.

You might also try another mode of meditation on *Shabbat.* Instead of programming your thoughts, you might, after some study, sit quietly, placing yourself in the Presence. Address God and say, "Please, give me a gift of insight today." Then, clear the mind from preoccupations with an act of offering-up your distractions.

Wait for God. There is no need to force any experience. It is enough to visit with God in silence, as one visits with a very good friend. One need not talk. There is a sort of trusting, *good-to-be-with-You,* quietude. If God wants to take it further, be grateful; but there is no need to force it. The mind will still be awash with all sorts of petty thoughts, which you will likely find difficult to banish.

Invite God to see into these thoughts, in the Presence they will hide. But to keep God's Presence in the mind is also difficult at first. After a while, thank the Holy One for being received with patience, and give your frustration as an offering to God. Then take the prayer-book and stand, perhaps swaying as you chant *Yah's* praises.

Don't just read in silence. Prayer is not about gaining new information. Address God in praise; or, if you can't feel yourself addressing God, address the world in its vastness, telling it of *Yah's* wonderful goodness. If you feel like injecting some of your own ideas of praise—in particular of God's kindness to us—by all means, do so.

After you have finished your prayers, and you sit down to eat, after having made the *Kiddush* and *Ha'Motzi* over the *hallah*, intend to feed God in your eating. Or reverse it and intend that God feeds you. Sing at the table, and between courses, talk about or think about an idea you have discovered in Torah. Psalm 23 is especially recommended for this.

The grace after meals is an especially rich time for *kavvanah*. Then, spend some time in study. Visualize God facing you and teaching you through the text. Say a short prayer of both petition for insight and thanksgiving for the opportunity of studying God's Will and Wisdom.

You will likely find that the *Shabbat* was all too short when you have to part from it on Saturday night. At *Havdalah*, the 'seperation,' we might ask that a spiritual 'hangover' linger into the coming week.

You can make your own particular *Shabbat* pattern that will fit into your specific interpersonal situation. The patterns of mealtime and prayer-observance by other members of the family have to be taken into consideration in planning the day. We might have to forsake quietude in order to be with others at home. But then you can always steer conversation into something valuable. You might tell a story, sing a *niggun*, or read an excerpt from a good book and begin to delve into it.

But a word of caution is in order. You mustn't give anyone in your family a reason to object to your search for God and thus turn the *Shabbat* into a battlefield. Remember that you are always free to 'intend' what you wish.

> If you live with friends who are with you in the endeavor, you might discuss it with them and plan ahead. Perhaps a retreat could be arranged on a *Shabbat*. At other times, any outward sign of devotion before others who are not with you in this is highly undesirable. There is plenty of room for this practice on the inside; structure *Shabbat* around our given situation.
>
> ∞

SEEING SHABBAT WITH THE EYES OF TOMORROW

VISION IS SEEING with the eyes of tomorrow. To open these eyes, one needs to transcend the pressure of the now. We speak of *Shabbat* as a small hologram of a future reality. Looking at *Shabbat* as a reality we would like to see seven years from now is helpful. We can then see what it is that we need to do in the intervening six years (or six days) to reach such a *Shabbat*.

Jews have good eyes for the past. Not only do we recall the past in our remembrances—*zekher l'ma'aseh be'reshit*, remembering the story of creation, and *zekher li'tziat mitzrayim,* remembering the story of our exodus from Egypt—we re-enact the times and seasons in our calendar. At times, we subtly restructure our memories in order to be able to keep the present and the past in reasonable touch. Thus, so much rabbinic *midrash,* or interpretation, sees scriptural events in rabbinic tableaux—e.g., David and the angel of death. The various *sedarim* we celebrate on *Pesah* are another instance of re-visioning the past for the present.

We have, when we wanted to see the future, projected the past ahead of us and prayed *hadeish yameinu k'kedem*, "renew our days as of old" (Lam. 5:21). Yet, in re-visioning the past, we are kept in the cycle of repeating it. Often when we look at the future, we project a nostalgia for the past and hope that it will be recreated for us—but without its problems. So we might envision a rebuilt Temple, offering the same sacrifices, but without the Romans and various sectaries. Yet, this won't work for us now as we embark upon a renewal of our faith. We need to start looking at the future in other ways.

Guidance:
Varieties of Shabbat Experience

I. ONE CANNOT always make *Shabbat* on all levels. When the body is tired, there is a *Shabbat* that reminds us of Egypt and bids us to rest—*pashut ke'mashema'o*, 'simply as it sounds'—in the most simple and concrete way. On the other hand, there may be the upwelling of hunger—not for bread or water, but—for God-words. There may be the homecoming to the warm haven, to family and one's emotional reference-group of beloveds. There, a *Shabbat* from loneliness and alienation can happen. Or, having dealt with a cognitive problem all week, one seeks a place with God-solitude, allowing the mind to rest in the trust that there are an abundance of solutions with which one can commune on *Shabbat* without mental exertion.

II. The *Shabbat* of just loafing: taking care of the body—focusing, relaxing, breathing, bathing, un-stressing, doing Tai Chi or Hatha Yoga; healing—meeting one's body as an ailing intimate friend in need of care, the

---

mammal resting in the para-sympathetic mode.

III. *Oneg Shabbat:* "Calling the Shabbat a delight" (Isa. 10:10) means that one ought to experience something that gives delight to both the soul and the body. While we have in our tradition exhortations to seek that delight for the body, there is also the expectation that there will be benefit accruing to the soul. Often these expectations in our tradition have pushed us to service the soul and we have not done enough for the body.

For the poor of the *shtetl,* 'good food' was turkey, quail and fish. There are some among us today who, from time-to-time, do a day of only juice, or only fruit, or enjoy a day of uncooked fruits and vegetables. It might become a custom to give the stomach a *Shabbat* from processed foods. On the other hand, if one does that regularly, or eats according to a careful diet regularly, the *Shabbat* might be a time to have something special, without overindulging.

The lawyer or broker who wears jeans on *Shabbat* is making a statement about rest. That person's *Shabbat* clothes are for loafing. Yet, when one seeks to enhance the delight of soul in solemn and momentous celebration of sacred values and focusing—special clothing is called for. A combination of comfort and ease with flair and drama makes for high ritual.

The Sefardim and Yemenites have as their *minhag,* or 'custom,' the preparation of fragrant flowers and herbs. Favorite fragrances for *Shabbat* moods can be set aside as we strive to create a personal *Gan Eden,* 'Garden of Eden.'

IV. Celebration: The neighborhood park may also be a marvelous locale for celebrating the seasons. Don't forget that dancing and singing are part of the traditional repertoire.

V. *Olam ha'Ba:* Consider a deep, silent retreat with a select group.

∞

OBEDIENCE AND CRITERIA FOR OBSERVANCE

THERE IS NO NEED here to go into detail about the particulars of your home observance and your business dealings. They are up to you and the kind of commitment you make. But it is important to consider 'how' you do so.

There is the intention of obedience. It makes little sense to wear yourself out in a selfish desire for inner growth for its own sake. With this motivation alone, no one survives the rigors of self-development. Some people only flirt with this for a little while before leaving it; but, in order to really progress, you need a different motivation, and that is loyal obedience to God.

This motivation, however, refuses to serve as a mere means to progress. One has to give in to the whole meaning of obedience and surrender one's own will for God's. In the course of being obedient, one can expect the real purpose of one's life to be achieved. While the servant image seems prosaic, and you might much rather see yourself as a child or lover of God, you will not really be able to relate to God as a child or lover unless, at least for a time, you have served God as a servant. When service in obedience is a real dimension in your life, you may afterward get 'orders' to move on to these other areas.

Obedience can be established in many ways. Here is one of them. And I think that until your commitment and thinking become clear, and the criteria of God's Will have become known to you, this one might be the best. Do you remember how you were asked to share this work with a friend? Hopefully, up to now, you have done this step by step, and here the friend becomes instrumental, as you will see:

GUIDANCE:

Listening for Marching Orders

AT PERIODS DURING THE DAY, listen a while for 'marching orders.' When you are sure of these orders, do not fail to carry them out. You must also, before listening, offer a short prayer for guidance, asking especially for criteria upon which to base checking these orders. Then, sit, empty yourself of thought, and jot down the orders you receive. As you proceed, you will see that they are not generally of a religious nature. They might have to do with some of the simpler things in life. But no one knows how they will be led; that is up to God.

There will be many times when you will be in doubt as to the origins of your orders. The simple way to check them is to see if the orders are not against (a broad reading of) the Ten Commandments. If you are still in doubt, check with your spiritual friend. When two friends talk about such matters, there are two inclinations for good fighting one inclination for evil.

As you proceed to follow your orders, send an intent of

---

added awareness toward God, offering your obedience with warm feelings. Find your own stirring term of endearment for God (this you need not even share with your friend) and, in addressing your thoughts, use the term mentally.

∞

This is what is meant by the acceptance of the heavenly yoke. It is borne when you fulfill your orders in both decision and action. You will find that in the measure you fulfill them, greater and higher tasks will eventually become yours. God has a way of bestowing little favors along the way which you will treasure.

Shalom

As it is about time to take leave of you, there are a few things you must still be told. You will need a teacher who will begin to direct you in details. You must learn to breathe again, to eat, drink, sleep, and so much more about how to pray. This teacher must get to know you as an individual, and prescribe for you in accord with your own physical type and psychological style.

By this time, you will also have discovered the 'ups and downs' of progress, the subtle shifts in moods, and the specially meaningful or meaningless things that are your very own. Books cannot help you much at this stage. But the teacher can. When you are really ready, you will find yourself directed to him or her. Of course, you must do a great deal of praying for this to happen. If it does not happen soon, this might be a sign that you still have to check your past progress. It is also possible that you will find a temporary teacher who will help you a bit further along the way, and then you will have to search again. Ultimately, you will find your true teacher.

Also, you must prepare yourself to be able to understand enough Hebrew to open yourself to further guidance within the Jewish tradition, allowing you to better take advantage of its *siddur* and Torah. And when you know some Hebrew, your teacher will have a deeper means of communication with your soul.

May God's Blessed Name be with you until you reach God's Self.

BEYOND I AND THOU

Yah, my God, where are You?
  I call You as if from afar,
  But You, my Redeemer,
  Dwell in my heart,
  So close, and I know it not.
Here You are,
  Present in my innermost,
  And so too at the outermost edge,
  Both my Source and Goal!
Where my feelings rise,
  There You are, stirring me,
  Nesting in the womb
  Of my very my urge.
Here in my eyes,
  You are the pupil,
  And I yearn so much
  To make of You
  The object of my sight.

My innards are pure,
>   Your sanctuary in me,
>   Sacred by Your Presence;
>   But how I long to scour them,
>   To make them worthy of the honor.

Show me how to host You,
>   Here in my body!
>   What a blessing!
>   Your nestling in my heart,

Life of my life,
>   You are with/in me
>   So how can I meet You
>   On the outside?

My song I would
>   Address to You
>   Were You beside me,
>   And not hidden in this voice.

Zoned in the point of knowing,
>   You hide in unseen splendor,
>   Glorious as I seek Your Glory;

Lingering on Your threshold,
>   My ego squats, claiming to be
>   The legal tenant of Your home.

More I cannot con-fuse
>   The two who shimmer
>   As one I-Am-ness;

Never can I leave this labyrinth
>   My self by myself.
>   Help me sortie and free me;
>   Then my prayer
>   Will be pure
>   For You.

Echo—
      Are You the call
      Or the answer?
      Even these words,
      Are they mine
      Or Yours?
Help and tell me,
      Love of my Heart,
      Are You not also
      The Love and the Heart?
Yah! God, adored One;
      I want to offer You
      A gift You will not spurn—
      Your will be mine—
      Is it not already so?
Holy solitude,
      All One Al-one,
      My sole One,
      My soul's One,
      My part(ner)
      My wholly,
      Holy Other,
      One.

      Amen.

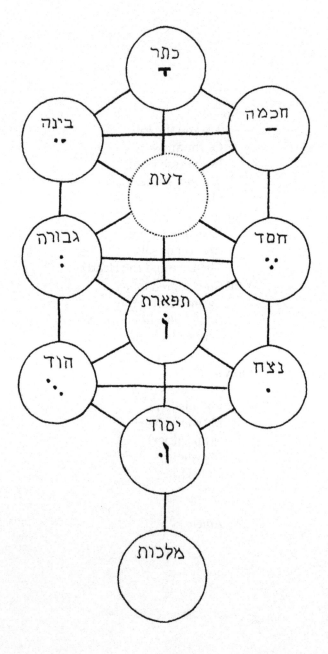

THE TREE OF LIFE &
THE DIVINE ATTRIBUTES

THROUGHOUT THIS MANUAL are various references to the *se'firot*, all of which relate to the spiritual structure called the Tree of Life, or *Etz Hayyim*. According to the Kabbalah, everything in creation reflects some combination of the 10 divine attributes or dimensions of reality that make up the Tree of Life. These 10 sefirot in descending order are *keter* (crown), which is utterly transcendent; *hokhmah* (wisdom), the seed containing the whole; *binah* (understanding), the detailed taxonomy of all the qualities inherent in the seed; *hesed* (loving-kindness), open expression; *ge'vurah* (strength), boundaries; *tiferet* (beauty), balancing openness and boundaries; *netzah* (victory), raw efficacy; *hod* (glory), aesthetic presentation; *yesod* (foundation), balancing efficacy and aesthetics; and *malkhut* (sovereignty), wholeness embodied.

The Tree of Life structure (shown on the facing page) reveals the significant relationship dynamics among the *se'firot*. The most basic of these dynamics are those defined by the Three Pillars of the Tree: The right-hand pillar—composed of *hokhmah, hesed,* and *netzah*—is the pillar of masculine attributes; the left-hand pillar—composed of *binah, ge'vurah,* and *hod*—is the pillar of the feminine attributes; and between them is the central pillar—composed of *keter, tiferet, yesod,* and *malkhut*—which is neutral and provides the balance to the polarities on either side.

— N.M-Y., editor.

S'firot Emanations	Attributes Of God	Days Of The Creation	Architypes Personified By:	Names Of That Aspect Of God	Body Parts Of Universal One	Cosmic Awareness World
Kether Crown	Enlightenment, All-Illuminating	Before Creation	Beyond Name And Form	"Ehyeh........ I Am.........	Crown Of The Head	Adam Kadmon
Hokhmah (Abba-Father)	Divine Wisdom	Before Creation	Beyond Name And Form	"Asher........ That.........	Right Of Brain	Azilut Emanation
Binah (Imma-Mother)	Divine Understanding	Before Creation	Beyond Name And Form	..."Ehyeh" ...I Am	Left Of Brain	B'riyah-Creation
Hesed Gedulah	Loving Kindness Grace	1st Day Sunday	Abraham-Male Miriam-Female	El	Right Arm	Y'Zirah Formation
Gevurah-Din	Justice, Rigor, Judgement	2nd Day Monday	Isaac-Male Leah-Female	ELoHYM	Left Arm	Y'zirah Formation
Tif'eret Rahamim	Beauty Mercy	3rd Day Tuesday	Jacob-Male Hannah-Female	YHVH	Heart Area	Y'zirah Formation
Nezah	Victory Eternity	4th Day Wednesday	Moses-Male Rebeccah-Female	ShaDday	Right Of Pelvis (Kidney, Thigh, Ovary, Testicle)	Spiritual Assiah Function
Hod	Glory	5th Day Thursday	Aaron-Male Sarah-Female	Zbaot	Left Of Pelvis (Kidney, Thigh, Ovary, Testicle)	Spiritual Assiah Function
Yesod	Foundation	6th Day Friday	Joseph-Male Tamar-Female	Yah	Genitals-Male, Also Tongue	Spiritual Assiah Function
Malkhut	Majesty Kingdom	7th Day Saturday	David-Male Rachel-Female	Adonay	Genitals-Female Also Mouth	Physical Assiah Function In Action

Cosmic Awareness World	S'firot Active	Torah Perception (Level of Holy Scripture)	Type Energy	Soul Aspect	Divine Name (Corresponding Parts)	Active Element	Realm	Faculty In Use
THE NO-THING • EYN SOF ABSOLUTE • BEYOND ALL WORLDS ZIMZUM • CONTRACTION • CREATION								
Adam Kadmon (first Man)	Kether (Crown)	Ineffable	Atik Kether Arikh	Yehidah (the unique single one)	Top Tip Of Yod	Quintessense Beyond Elements	Ideal Of God	Delight Will Desire
Azilut (emanation)	Hokhmah (Divine Wisdom)	Sod Comprehension of the mystery	All S'firot present	Hayah (The Living One)	Head Of The Yod	Fire	Human Ideal	Divine Intellect
PARSAH • EGO BARRIER • NO OBJECT OF CREATION CAN PASS • TRANSCENDENCE DOOR								
B'riyah (creation)	Binah	D'rush-Search (Inductive Awareness)	Seraphim (angelic energy form of thought)	Neshamah	First Hay In God's Name	Air (for Breathing)	Animal Ideal	Thought
Y'zirah (formation)	S'firot	Remez-hint (deductive)	Hayot (chariot animals)	Ru'ah (Spirit of man)	The Vav Of His Name	Water	Plant Ideal	Feeling Speech Song
Assiah (function)	Malkhut	P'shat-divested (simple)	Ofanim (wheels)	Nefesh	Last Hay	Earth	Mineral Ideal	Action
Physical Assiah (function in the world of action)		Grammar (Mechanics)	Electro-Magnetic Spectrum of Matter	Physical Body	In The Name	Earth	Mineral	Action

	Friday Night Meal and Prayers	Sabbath A.M.	Sabbath P.M.	Saturday Night
The archetypal person in ascendancy	Abraham Grace Generosity Hospitality Immanence First Temple Thesis	Isaac Rigor and intensity Profundity Ideological clarity Second Temple Antithesis	Jacob Mercy, beauty Integrity Third Messianic Temple Synthesis	"David King of Israel alive existing" Majesty
Antagonists and dangers	Ishmael Idolatry Fertility cult Hospitality without discrimination	Esau Divisiveness Baseless hatred	None All Jacob's children Israelites	
From the *Zobar* and from the writings of Rabbi Isaac Luria (16th century)	Shekhinah or feminine aspect of God "Holy orchard" Lower paradise Holy wedding: union of heh, vav, and heh	"Ancient of Days" "Eyn-Sof" Transcendent aspect of God Upper paradise God withdrawn into His yod	The impatient lover Masculine aspect Paradise on earth God immanent in redemptive strivings Vav	Shekhinah extending sustenance for next week Adny
From *The Star of Redemption*, Franz Rosenzweig (1887-1929) Services	Creation "in remembrance of the act of creation"	Revelation "Moses rejoiced" The Sinai-gift	Redemption "And the Redeemer will come to Zion" "Jacob and his children rest theron"	"Into Life"
Relation	Divine-World	Divine-Man	Man-World	Integration of two triangles
Meal celebrates primarily	Israel	Torah	God	

	Friday Night Meal and Prayers	Sabbath A.M.	Sabbath P.M.	Saturday Night
Mood and setting	Gentle, expansive At home Eating with much singing (¾ time) Great variety of food Celebrating the body All together Open joy Love talk Japa-Bhakti	Quiet, reflective intellectual Reviewing history sub specie aeternitatis Teaching Torah Stately melodies (4/4 time) Calm, head-joy Cholent and kugel Contemplation Jnana	Yearning, longing Torah-dreaming about the good life Melody: slow and recitative Food: meager and in the synagogue Togetherness Tarrying Preparation of motivation for action Karma	Hopeful Story, ballad In group at shul or at one home to which all come Relaxed and buoyant The fellowship of comrades Lila
Intentions	Homecoming Transformation from dog to prince Nostalgia The haven of the old way Harmony in the home (candles) Past	Awakening to unchanging realities God is all; He is "the soul of all that lives" The perfect order un-impeded Ever-Present	Realization of what correction is needed Celebration of man's inherent possibility "None is like your people Israel, one nation on earth" Present-Future	Charge up week-day resources Seek vision of Elijah and his help and advice in involvement in world
Program	Recovering the good past History, patri-archs The Lord Was King	Anchoring the essential self in unchanging trans-cendence Millennium Messiah The Lord Is King	Promise of possible correction Seek God's will: in the present, e.g. in ecology, in technology The Lord Will Be King	Specific action directives to further God's kingdom on earth

REFLECTION:
On Philosophy & Theology

WHEN YOU FIRST BEGIN to pray seriously, you are often met by the questions of philosophy. What is prayer all about? Why pray? Doesn't God know what I wish to say already? What does it accomplish? Then the even weightier questions: Who is God? What is God? Does God exist? And even more pressing questions: If there is a God, how can there be evil?

The temptation is to try to solve these eternal questions as they arise, making sure that all the answers are in place before continuing the work of developing the spirit. But this temptation is best avoided. You need to realize that the left-brained way of analysis and reasoning is, at best, only going to lead to a fine, static God-idea, and not to the living God. Once a believer is committed to a belief, they begin to formulate a theology; but it must be borne in mind that theology is only the afterthought of the believer. The immediate and personal, as well as the social experience of a person, precedes the formulation. Furthermore, any formulation that can be given in words *will not do*, since words can at best contain only up to 180 degrees of the truth, which itself is 360 degrees. The God-Truth is *at least* 360 degrees.

How can we wait until all of the evidence is in? It is not by further refinement of our one-sided abstractions about God that we will come to true understanding. All that is required is a simple working hypothesis. This appears as follows:

> There have been some people in the world who have taken the spiritual path. As they reported on their experiences and realizations, there was gathered

a great cumulative mass of testimony about their experiences with God, and by others who related to them and witnessed that these people had led lives of special significance and holiness.

Ask yourself: Was it not this basic hypothesis that first led you to the spiritual path? You reasoned that taking a path similar to those who achieved some higher level of awareness, and who shared this path with others, would also allow you to touch that holy dimension. So wait with your theology until you too have some of your own spiritual experiences and then go ahead and use your theology as an afterthought, making sayable sense of them. Then, philosophy will be of use in showing you the structure of your theology.

It is in the nature of our inner-being that there is a distortion of the divine clarity, allowing us to see the truth only when presented in terms of that distortion. As it says in the Talmud: prior to birth, we are instructed in the womb by the angel who teaches us Torah. But this knowledge is shocked into amnesia at birth. So the Rabbis ask, "Why did the angel teach you in the first place if you have to forget what you learned?" The answer given is that all your subsequent study will lead you to say, *"A-ha!* I knew it all along!" (Niddah 30b)

So why does one have to have a special angel assigned to teach us? Because no one else's philosophy can quite satisfy your soul; therefore, the angel has to teach you according to the source of your unique soul. Certainty is not the result of having heard someone else say something, or having read someone else's writing; certainty results from being aware of how the soul connects its insight, as it is now experienced in reality, with the truth recalled on the inner-soul-plane of the angel's instruction.

In this way, the soul knows the truth that the mind tries to map. And in this way a person can draw a reality-map on which to base everyday decisions. This map is subject to constant revision by new experiences resonating with the inner intuition. In-tuition—inner teaching, the tuition on the inside—is another way of saying what the midrashic image is trying to convey. When this map is static, it becomes rapidly outdated.

So, when you experience the contradictions of philosophies in the inner work, don't let it trouble you. There is time for doing the philosophical homework twice a year: during the vernal and autumnal equinoxes and the periods before and around the full moons nearest to them—in the liturgical settings of Passover and the High Holy Days. One needs a summer-dew philosophy and a winter-rain/snow philosophy. Philosophies worked-out during the Winter and Summer solstices don't have staying-power and reality-rootedness. They are either too manic (summery) or too depressed (wintery). Both the metaphorical and the real-time periods are meant.

Besides, all philosophies are somehow and somewhere true for a while and for a given situation. The soul can get in touch with these momentary perspectives in meditation. The one who believes God is a person, and the one who believes that God is *beyond* personhood, are both right, each for a different phase of the work. The loving devotee will find it easier to serve God, the Person-Transcendent, and the people-helpers will find it easier to serve God-Immanent in the recipient of the help. Each one verifies from their own perspective the proof of the universe of discourse with which they most often work. The *doer* finds that what *works* is true. The *feeler* believes truth because it *feels* right. The *thinker* sees that their ideas are coherent and have no inner contradictions; one who participates in this knows truth by self-realization. We are made in the image of God whose four-lettered Name—*Y-H-V-H*—points to all four levels at once.

So it is the glory of the way of the spirit in Judaism not to demand this or that philosophy as if it were the static, once-and-for-all, definitive one. The philosophical work needs to be heuristic and *ad hoc*. In this way, each day of the Counting of the Omer, the 'measuring' taking place after Passover, has a philosophy of its own to be worked with and through in the approach to Sinai and a fruitful revelation. Each of the week's *sidrot*, or Torah portions, also has its own time and consciousness texture. One who lives the *sidrot* in all their shades and hues prepares for a multifaceted revelation.

Which philosophy is right? A Hasid would respond to this question with another—"When and Where?" Deism is the lesson of the material universe. Theism is the lesson of the spiritual worlds. Pantheism is the lesson of the times of the Messiah—the unitive theophany at the end of time is the experience of the resurrection and the Sabbatical Millenium. All of these are at times accessible, even here on this plane—if not fully, then at least as reflected in us. The holy days and seasons align us differently to states of being and their corresponding philosophies.

The kabbalists teach us that each moment carries within itself another permutation of the Divine Name. Even such matters as God as person or beyond are not static concepts. God is for us feminine each *Erev Shabbat,* Sabbath Eve, and transcendent-transpersonal *Shabbat* morning, and intensely personal and impatient for redemption on *Shabbat* afternoon. So, if the language of the prayer-book or the Bible creates cognitive problems, take the initiative and give it the best possible interpretation you can; change the metaphors from "Father" and "King" and "God" to "She" or "It" or "Friend," or to pronouns that suit the needs of your soul at this time. Don't wrestle with the concepts. Under guidance you can explore the special energies inherent in the Divine Names and metaphors that are the interfaces between the finite and the infinite.

∞

Recommendations
for Further Reading

Buber, Martin. *For the Sake of Heaven.* Tr. Ludwig Lewisohn. Philadelphia: The Jewish Publication Society of America, 1945.

—. *Tales of the Hasidim: The Early Masters.* Tr. Olga Marx. New York: Schocken Books, 1947.

—. *Tales of the Hasidim: The Later Masters.* Tr. Olga Marx. New York: Schocken Books, 1947.

—. *Ten Rungs: Hasidic Sayings.* Tr. Olga Marx. New York: Schocken Books, 1947.

—. *The Way of Man: According to the Teaching of Hasidism.* New York: The Citadel Press, 1967.

Buxbaum, Yitzhak. *Jewish Spiritual Practices.* Northvale, NJ: Jason Aronson Press, 1990.

—. *The Light and Fire of the Baal Shem Tov.* New York: Continuum, 2005.

Cooper, David A.. *Entering the Sacred Mountain: A Mystical Odyssey.* New York: Bell Tower, 1994.

—. *God is a Verb: Kabbalah and the Practice of Mystical Judaism.* New York: Riverhead Books, 1997.

Ekstein, Menachem. *Visions of a Compassionate World: Guided Imagery for Spiritual Growth and Social Transformation.* Tr. Yehoshua Starrett. New York: Urim Publications, 2001.

Firestone, Tirzah. *The Receiving: Reclaiming Jewish Women's Wisdom.* San Francisco: HarperSanFrancisco, 2003.

Green, Arthur. *Ehyeh: A Kabbalah for Tomorrow.* Woodstock, VT: Jewish Lights Publishing, 2003.

—. *Radical Judaism: Rethinking God and Tradition.* New Haven,

CT: Yale University Press, 2010.

Green, Arthur, and Barry W. Holtz (ed. & tr.) *Your Word is Fire: The Hasidic Masters on Contemplative Prayer*. Woodstock, VT: Jewish Lights Publishing, 1993.

Green, Arthur, with Ebn Leader, Ariel Evan Mayse, Or N. Rose (ed. & tr.) *Speaking Torah: Spiritual Teachings from Around the Maggid's Table: Volume I*. Woodstock, VT: Jewish Lights Publishing, 2013.

—. *Speaking Torah: Spiritual Teachings from Around the Maggid's Table: Volume II*. Woodstock, VT: Jewish Lights Publishing, 2013.

Heschel, Abraham Joshua. *Human—God's Ineffable Name*. Tr. Zalman Schachter-Shalomi. Boulder, CO: Albion-Andalus Books, 2012.

—. *Man's Quest for God: Studies in Prayer and Symbolism*. Aurora Press, 1998.

—. *The Sabbath*. New York: Farrar Straus Giroux, 2005.

Kagan, Michael. *The King's Messenger: A Parable of Judaism*. Boulder, CO: Albion-Andalus Books, 2013.

Kantrowitz, Min. *Counting the Omer: A Kabbalistic Meditation Guide*, Santa Fe, NM: Gaon Books, 2009.

Kaplan, Aryeh. *Innerspace: Introduction to Kabbalah, Meditation and Prophecy*. Ed. Avraham Sutton. Brooklyn. Moznaim, 1991.

—. *Jewish Meditation: A Practical Guide*. New York: Schocken Books, 1985.

—. *Meditation and Kabbalah*. York Beach, ME: Samuel Weiser, 1982.

—. *Meditation and the Bible*. York Beach, ME: Samuel Weiser, 1978.

Kushner, Lawrence. *The Book of Words*. Woodstock, VT: Jewish Lights Publishing, 1993.

—. *God was in This Place and I, I Did Not Know*. Woodstock, VT: Jewish Lights Publishing, 1991.

—. *The River of Light: Spirituality, Judaism and the Evolution of Consciousness*. San Francisco: Harper & Row, 1981.

Moshe Leib of Sassov. *A Guide to Spiritual Progress*. Tr. Zalman Schachter-Shalomi. Boulder, CO: Albion-Andalus Books, 2012.

Nachman of Breslov. *Outpouring of the Soul: Rabbi Nachman's Path in Meditation*. Tr. Aryeh Kaplan. Monsey, NY: Breslov Research Institute, 1980.

—. *Restore My Soul! Meshivat Nefesh*. Tr. Avraham Greenbaum. Monsey, NY: Breslov Research Institute, 1980.

Nahman of Bratzlav. *Tale of the Seven Beggars*. Tr. Zalman Schachter-Shalomi. Boulder, CO: Albion-Andalus Books, 2010.

Novick, Leah. *On the Wings of Shekhinah: Rediscovering Judaism's Divine Feminine*. Quest Books, 2008.

Prager, Marcia. *The Path of Blessing: Experiencing the Energy and Abundance of the Divine*. New York: Bell Tower, 1998.

Raphael, Simcha Paull. *Jewish Views of the Afterlife*. Northvale, NJ: Jason Aronson, 1994.

Rose, Or, with Ebn D. Leader. *God in All Moments: Mystical and Practical Wisdom from Hasidic Masters*. Woodstock, VT: Jewish Lights Publishing, 2003.

Roth, Jeff. *Jewish Meditation Practices for Everyday Life: Awakening Your Heart, Connecting with God*. Woodstock, VT: Jewish Lights Publishing, 2009.

Schachter-Shalomi, Zalman. *All Breathing Life Adores Your Name: At the Interface Between Poetry and Prayer*. Ed. Michael L. Kagan. Santa Fe, NM: Gaon Books, 2011.

—. *The Gates of Prayer: Twelve Talks on Davvenology*. Boulder, CO: Albion-Andalus Books, 2011.

—. *Geologist of the Soul: Talks on Rebbe-craft and Spiritual Leadership*. Boulder, CO: Albion-Andalus Books, 2012.

— (tr.). *Sh'ma': A Concise Weekday Siddur for Praying in English*. Boulder, CO: Albion-Andalus Books, 2010.

— (tr.). *Tikkun Klali: Rebbe Nahman of Bratzlav's Ten Remedies of the Soul*. Boulder, CO: Albion-Andalus Books, 2013.

Schachter-Shalomi, Zalman, and Yair Hillel Goelman (ed. & tr.). *Ahron's Heart: The Prayers, Teachings and Letters of Ahrele Roth, A Hasidic Reformer*. Teaneck, NJ: Ben Yehuda Press, 2009.

Schachter-Shalomi, Zalman, with Donald Gropman. *First Steps to a New Jewish Spirit: Reb Zalman's Guide to Recapturing the Intimacy and Ecstasy in Your Relationship with God*. Woodstock, VT: Jewish Lights Publishing, 2003.

Schachter-Shalomi, Zalman, and Netanel Miles-Yépez. *God Hidden, Whereabouts Unknown: An Essay on the 'Contraction' of God in Different Jewish Paradigms*. Boulder, CO: Albion-Andalus Books, 2013.

—. *A Heart Afire: Stories and Teachings of the Early Hasidic Masters*. Philadelphia: Jewish Publication Society, 2009.

—. *A Hidden Light: Stories and Teachings of Early HaBaD and Bratzlav Hasidism*, Santa Fe, NM: Gaon Books, 2011.

—. *A Merciful God: Stories and Teachings of the Holy Rebbe, Levi Yitzhak of Berditchev*. Boulder, CO: Albion-Andalus Books, 2010.

Schachter-Shalomi, Zalman, with Joel Segel. *Davening: A Guide to Meaningful Jewish Prayer*. Woodstock, VT: Jewish Lights Publishing, 2012.

—. *Jewish with Feeling: A Guide to Meaningful Jewish Practice*. New York: Riverhead Books, 2005.

Schachter-Shalomi, Zalman, with Daniel Siegel. *Credo of a Modern Kabbalist*. Victoria, BC: Trafford Publishing, 2005.

—. *Integral Halachah: Transcending and Including*. Victoria, BC: Trafford Publishing, 2007.

Schneersohn, Yosef Yitzchak. *Saying Tehillim: On the Subject of Reciting Psalms*. Tr. Zalman I. Posner. Brooklyn, NY: Kehot Publication Society, 2000.

Shainberg, Catherine. *Kabbalah and the Power of Dreaming: Awakening the Visionary Life*. Rochester, VT: Inner Traditions, 2005.

Shapira, Kalonymus Kalman. *Conscious Community: A Guide to Inner Work.* Tr. Andrea Cohen-Kiener. Northvale, NJ: Jason Aronson, 1999.

benShea, Noah. *Jacob the Baker.* Number Nine Media, 2013.

Sheinkin, David. *Path of the Kabbalah.* New York: Paragon House, 1998.

Steinsaltz, Adin. *A Guide to Jewish Prayer,* New York: Schocken Books, 2000.

—. *The Long Shorter Way: Discourses on Chasidic Thought.* Tr. Yehuda Hanegbi. Northvale, NJ: Jason Aronson, 1988.

—. *The Thirteen Petalled Rose.* Tr. Yehuda Hanegbi. Northvale, NJ: Jason Aronson, 1992.

Waskow, Arthur. *Seasons of Our Joy: A Modern Guide to the Jewish Holidays.* Philadelphia, PA: Jewish Publication Society, 2012.

Wiesel, Elie. *Souls on Fire: Portraits and Legends of Hasidic Masters.* Tr. Marion Wiesel. New York: Random House, 1972.

Gate to the Heart

Rabbi Zalman Schachter-Shalomi, better known as 'Reb Zalman,' was born in Zholkiew, Poland, in 1924. His family fled the Nazi oppression in 1938 and finally landed in New York City in 1941. Descended from a distinguished family of Belzer Hasidim, he became a Habad Hasid as a teenager while still living in Antwerp, Belgium. He was later ordained by Habad-Lubavitch in 1947 and became one of the Lubavitcher Rebbe's first generation of outreach workers. He later earned his MA in psychology from Boston University in 1956 and a DHL from Hebrew Union College in 1968. He is professor emeritus of Psychology of Religion and Jewish Mysticism at Temple University and is World Wisdom Chair holder emeritus at Naropa University. Today he is primarily known as the Rebbe and father of the Jewish Renewal movement, and is widely considered one of the world's foremost authorities on Hasidism and Kabbalah. He is the author of *Spiritual Intimacy: A Study of Counseling in Hasidism* (1991), *Jewish with Feeling: Guide to a Meaningful Jewish Practice* (2005), co-author of *A Heart Afire: Stories and Teachings of the Early Hasidic Masters* (2009).